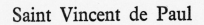

Saint Vincent de Paul

Saint Vincent de Paul

by

M. V. WOODGATE

THE NEWMAN PRESS
WESTMINSTER   MARYLAND

NIHIL OBSTAT:

IOSEPHUS A. CARROLL,
CENSOR THEOL. DEPUT.

DUBLINI, DIE 15ᵃ JANUARII, 1958.

IMPRIMI POTEST:

✠ IOANNES CAROLUS,
ARCHIEP. DUBLINEN.,
HIBERNIAE PRIMAS.

First Published 1958
Reprinted   1960

PRINTED IN THE REPUBLIC OF IRELAND
BY BROWNE & NOLAN, LTD., DUBLIN

Letters of Vincent de Paul, his Conferences, various contemporary histories and biographies, besides other publications of more recent date have been used in the compilation of this volume. But that which has been used the most, and without which it could not have been written, is the great life of Saint Vincent de Paul by Pierre Coste—himself a member of the Congregation of Mission Priests, founded over three hundred years ago in Paris.

M. V. W.

CONTENTS

CHAPTER I

Captivity and Freedom

ON a September morning of the year 1605 the people of Tunis witnessed a somewhat unusual sight—that of a group of Frenchmen with chains about their necks being paraded through their streets. The men had been captured a few days previously by Turkish pirates and were shortly to be put up to auction. Appraising as well as curious eyes followed them.

Amongst the little group stood out one figure, a tall, slight Gascon, strong and muscular, very good-looking. He was a priest, Vincent de Paul by name and his sale took place quite soon. A fisherman bought him, then quickly re-sold him to an old alchemist. The young man was to remain in slavery for some two years.

The incident was a curious one and did not fit in with the pattern of his previous life, which had been quietly uneventful, though marked by more than a usual amount of success. Indeed, from his earliest years success had come to him with remarkable ease. He had never known failure, and his future, it seemed safe to predict, would be successful too. But now, in a moment, all was changed and he was faced by slavery in a heathen, hostile country.

He was twenty-four at the time, having been born in 1581. His birthplace was a village of southern France not far from Dax in the neighbourhood of Toulouse. He came of a good, old peasant stock, his father being the owner of a small farm, all the work of which he did himself, helped by his wife and family of six children. Vincent was the third of the family, and care of the animals fell to him. Barefoot he would wander over the fields and hills, though his mind, already eager and intelligent, was occupied with other things than the flocks he guarded. His intelligence, indeed, was so keen that when

he was twelve years old, his father arranged for him to go
to school in Dax, an action which was not wholly disinterested.
For with education as well as intelligence, the boy might
some day become a priest, and as a priest he would be able to
help his family in many ways. Ambition was strong in
Vincent's father, and was equally strong in Vincent at this
time.

Eagerly he fell in with his father's plan, though he was
irked by the knowledge that the carrying out of it would
involve his family in an outlay of money which they could ill
afford. The fees for his schooling, however, were soon
reduced by his own industry, for, soaring ahead of his fellow-
pupils, a moment came when he—while still pursuing his
own studies—was able to earn money by teaching. He was
appointed tutor to the children of the resident magistrate of
the district, a certain Monsieur de Comet, who was from the
first greatly attracted by the brilliant peasant boy. Vincent
was made part of Monsieur de Comet's family, and the elder
man encouraged him in the idea that his studies should lead
him to the priesthood.

These years at Dax were very happy for Vincent. He loved
his work and was so well liked and popular amongst all who
knew him that memory of his humble home began to grow
dim. He did not want to think about it, having become
faintly ashamed of it and of his parents. One day when his
father arrived to visit him, dressed in his rough peasant
clothes, the boy could hardly bring himself to speak to him,
conduct which must have hurt the older man. Yet it made
no difference to his treatment of his son, for we presently
hear of the sale of two oxen to enable the boy to go to college
at Toulouse. There he remained until 1600, when he was
ordained priest at the early age of nineteen. Again, he supple-
mented by teaching the expenses of his education, which
were actually so considerable that he was obliged to run into
debt to meet them. The risk involved by such debt, however,
was not great for one of his youth and gifts.

The fact of his ordination he took with a seriousness
unusual in his day, and it was with awe that he looked forward
to the saying of his first Mass. " He trembled at the thought
of his own unworthiness." He would not say it in Toulouse,

nor yet at Dax, but chose instead a tiny chapel hidden far away on a neighbouring hillside, only another priest and a server being his companions.

He returned from it to Toulouse and there resumed at once his previous studies and his teaching. His priesthood had done little outwardly to change his life. He did no pastoral work, but opened instead a school for the sons of " the nobility and gentry " of the district round. This proved so successful that it made him soon something of a marked man in the city.

Then at the beginning of the year 1605—the same which saw him later being paraded through the streets of Tunis— he was summoned by the ducal uncle of two of his pupils to Bordeaux to talk about a new appointment. The appoint- ment was so important that the heavy expenses of the journey it involved seemed well justified to him, and all the more so, when on his return to Toulouse, he learned that an old lady of his acquaintance in the city had died leaving him her fortune.

This news, however, was not so wonderful as it appeared at first, since " a good-for-nothing, worthless scamp," as Vincent described him, had managed to steal the greater part of the legacy, and was living on it very happily at Marseilles. There was nothing for Vincent to do but to go after him, which he did without delay. The " scamp " was arrested, thrown into prison and the sum of three hundred crowns extracted from him by Vincent, who was about to turn back in triumph to Toulouse, when it was suggested to him that instead of going there by land, as he had come, he should go by sea. Here was a cheaper form of travel, and it was also quicker. So with no thought in his mind of what this seem- ingly unimportant decision was to make to him, he stepped on board a vessel which was to bring him home.

The weather was perfect, the wind favourable, everything was going well, when three pirate ships were sighted, and thereafter Vincent's life was changed. The pirates boarded his small craft, several of the crew and passengers were killed and the rest put into irons to be conveyed to Tunis. Vincent himself was wounded in the leg with a wound which never ceased to trouble him. A rough dressing, however, healed it sufficiently for it to detract nothing from his value when the moment came for him to be paraded round those burning Tunisian streets, the scene of which he thus describes himself.

"After making us march five or six times round the city, the ruffians brought us back to the ship so that the merchants might see those who could eat heartily and those who could not, and thus show that our wounds were not mortal. They then brought us back to the market-place, to which the merchants came to examine us, just as one does when buying a horse or an ox. They made us open our mouths and show our teeth, felt our sides, examined our wounds, made us walk, trot and run. They then made us carry loads and wrestle, that they might gauge the strength of each individual, beside a thousand other brutalities."

This nightmare procedure ended for Vincent only with his sale, though his heart doubtless failed him when he realised that it was a fisherman who had bought him, for he hated the sea. Such hatred must have been quickly apparent, for the fisherman lost no time in re-selling him. His new owner— the Mahometan alchemist—was well pleased with him, seeing in so well made and powerful a youth one who would be invaluable to him in the stoking of his furnaces.

A touch of the fantastic may here be noted. Who in Dax or in Toulouse would be able to imagine Vincent the victim of such an extraordinary adventure? One moment a grave young priest, engaged in teaching and study, a future of the fairest opening out before him—the next lost to all in a pagan country, slave to an old magician! Nobody knew anything about him. The pirates had described him as a Spaniard. Escape was impossible. He had no choice but to submit to his most tragic fate, for tragic it assuredly was. The high hopes which his visit to Bordeaux had brought him were now all dashed. His school must come to an end, together with his studies. He was left with absolutely nothing, not even his own clothes.

And yet his fate could have been worse, as he was quick to realise himself. For his new master proved kindly, and indeed, gave him quite soon the most surprising affection. " He was very fond of me," writes Vincent, " and took pleasure in discoursing to me on alchemy, and still more on his religion, to which he bent all his efforts to win me, promising me abundant riches and all his knowledge."

The old man's religion awakened no interest in Vincent, but his most peculiar knowledge quickly did, and with lively Gascon curiosity aroused, Vincent would watch entranced all the experiments daily taking place beneath his eyes. The old man could, for instance, transform silver into gold quite easily. " I often saw him melt down equal quantities of gold and silver, first arranging them in thin layers, over which he put a layer of some powders, then another layer of the metals, and finally another layer of powders. He then put the lot into a melting-pot or goldsmith's crucible and placed them in a furnace for twenty-four hours. After which time he opened the furnace and the silver had become gold."

He knew many strange conjuring tricks. He could make a skull appear to speak, and was master of other unusual knowledge, all the secrets of which he was delighted to share with Vincent. For nearly a year Vincent served him, then the old man being summoned away for a visit to the Grand Sultan of Turkey, Vincent was put up to auction again. This time he was bought by a Savoyard, a native of Nice, who had abjured his faith and nationality and was living with three wives in the mountains near.

One of these wives, an intelligent Greek, who knew already something of Christianity, was attracted immediately by Vincent and would stand beside him for long hours as he dug in the fields, questioning him about his religion. Sometimes he would sing psalms to her, or the *Salve Regina*. " It was quite marvellous to see the delight she took in all this," he wrote, " and she did not fail to tell her husband in the evening that he had done wrong in abandoning his religion, which she considered an extremely good one." And through her influence and that of Vincent, the Savoyard at last began to see it as " an extremely good one " too. So much so, that he started to repent of his apostasy, and after Vincent had been with him for ten months arranged to escape with the young man to France.

Of the details of that escape we know nothing beyond that it was affected in " a little skiff," which landed the two at

Aigues-Mortes, from which they proceeded to Avignon. And at Avignon Vincent, finding a gentleman who was on his way to Toulouse, immediately sat down and wrote a letter to Monsieur de Comet containing a history of his adventure. The letter described also the joy with which Vincent's companion was received back into the Church by the Vice-Legate of Avignon. The latter was deeply interested in the two, as well he might be. He even arranged for them to accompany him to Rome whither he was going on a visit. " He honours me with his affection and desires my preferment," wrote Vincent.

Vincent was now twenty-six. He had had a remarkable experience, which he who was gifted with Gasçon wit and humour, and who was, moreover, a natural mimic, could turn into an exciting story. But it was a story which, oddly enough, the Vice-Legate did not want him to share with anybody else. All the strange secrets which Vincent had learned from the old magician, his conjuring tricks " and a thousand other beautiful and geometrical matters which he taught me," Vincent wrote from Rome, " these His Lordship is so jealous of that he does not wish me to meet anybody, lest I should teach them, for he desires that he alone may have the reputation of knowing these matters, which he is sometimes pleased to exhibit before His Holiness and the Cardinals." A curious little picture is conjured up by the words—Pope and hierarchy listening gravely to the secrets of an old magician and watching gravely the magician's tricks as performed by Vincent's friend!

Vincent's visit to Rome lasted for only a few months, during which time he continued his theological studies and learned Italian. He also steeped himself in the loveliness of Rome, and emotional always, would sometimes be moved to tears as his powerful imagination re-created scenes which had happened within its walls. He left Italy at last some time during 1608 and returned to France, going at once to Paris, a city which he had never visited before.

CHAPTER II

Paris

HE was twenty-eight and his future was not hopeful. The debts which he had contracted at Dax and Toulouse remained, and he had no money with which to meet them. He had been living while in Rome on the bounty of the Savoyard. Those in France who had wanted to help him before had now mostly forgotten him. His father was dead, and he could not in all decency ask further aid of a family which had taxed themselves already so much for him. His one idea, therefore, was to settle into some " honest benefice " where he could live in peace, while aiding his family so far as in him lay. All ambition, any idea of success or fame, which might have been his in the past, had long since left him, killed by his Turkish captors, who had changed not only his life, but his character as well. His eyes were opened now, as never before, to suffering, to the pitilessness of the world and to the agony of being defenceless. He had learned also something of physical pain. How would he, who was more perceptive and more sensitive than most react to these experiences? Nobody could know, and few were interested enough to wonder as he arrived in Paris unknown, penniless and friendless. But he would not remain friendless long. He was adaptable. His life had already revealed him as possessor of a charm which was so great that it could reach from French " nobility and gentry " to a Mahometan alchemist, and the highest of church dignitaries. His interest in others, his sympathy for them, and his power of transporting himself into their lives made up a large part of this charm. A great, if unconscious, selflessness was already his.

The Paris he found was full of scintillating life. Henri IV,

the one-time Huguenot King of Navarre, and now the most
beloved monarch France has ever had, was reigning. His
first marriage with *la Reine Margot*, the beautiful, profligate
sister of the late King, had been dissolved, and he was married
to the Italian, Marie de Medici, who had already borne him
two sons. Wise rulership and a wise chancellor had brought
a period of prosperity to the country, the people of which
Henri really cared for. And with this material revival had
come a spiritual one as well, which has been accounted the
greatest ever known in France. Henri Bremond describes
it as " the golden age of our religious history." And the
leader of it was a man named Pierre de Bérulle, soon to be a
cardinal, not widely known in his own day and little known
now, even though he was accounted then and has been considered since one of the great masters of the spiritual life.
Beneath his influence Vincent was to fall, to be moulded—
though only very gradually—into the saint which he would
eventually become.

De Bérulle was at the time a man of thirty-five and thus a
few years older than Vincent. He belonged to Paris and came
of an intellectual family, of which he himself was the most
learned member. " In appearance," we are told, " he was
small and insignificant, gentle and even yielding." He had,
nevertheless, a " master mind."

Early ordained priest, he early made a complete revolution
in the spiritual thought of his day. Yet, acute theologian
though he was, his message to those who came to him for
direction was one of simplicity. " First of all it is needful to
regard God and not oneself," he wrote, " not to act by any
regard or desire of oneself, but only by the pure regard of
God." " My sisters," he wrote to some Carmelite nuns, " you
should all of you fix your gaze incessantly on Jesus, living
only in and for Him. You should be nought but a pure
capacity of Him, clinging to Him, filled with Him, breathing
nought but His spirit and His grace." " He was so greatly
filled with our Lord Jesus Christ," is noted by one who knew
him, " that his love welled like a torrent over him, and it was
to Him that he sent all those disciples thrown in his way by
Providence." Many disciples were thrown in his way, though
the most illustrious of them all was Vincent de Paul, the lonely

young priest who, having just arrived in Paris, approached him with great diffidence.

How Vincent came to hear of him we do not know, nor yet the first impression which each made upon the other. But de Bérulle was ready to help him, and there were few assuredly in Paris who needed help as much as he did.

No previous spiritual influence had touched him closely up till now, nor had he ever encountered anyone resembling de Bérulle in the least. He seems to have had actually little spiritual help of any kind in his life. He had neither sought for it, nor desired it, but with a detached, impersonal spirit had pursued alone his quiet way—at home, at Dax, at Toulouse, later in Africa, even in Rome.

He was so poor on his first arrival in the capital that he was obliged to share a room with another man, a young lawyer from Bordeaux. The two got on well together until a miserable incident occurred. A boy, sent to deliver some medicines to Vincent, stole a large sum of money belonging to the lawyer, who at once accused Vincent of the theft. Vincent's denials he would not accept. He proclaimed Vincent a thief wherever he went, and it was only after six years had elapsed that the real culprit confessed what he had done.

Here was an incident to cloud the outlook of any young man anxious to make a new life for himself. Another was to follow on a different plane, but bringing with it even more searching distress. Some work Vincent had been given to do at a neighbouring hospital brought him into contact with a priest who had lost his faith and was passing through great agony in consequence. Nothing that Vincent could say to him made any difference and, the man having got to a point where Vincent feared his suicide, Vincent offered before God to take upon himself his anguish. The offering was accepted. The other's faith was restored, but Vincent's own was taken from him. " Night invaded his soul " and continued to reign there for some considerable time. Prayer and mortification availed nothing, and only as Vincent was inspired one day to make the absolutely sincere surrender of his whole life to the service of the poor did faith return to him, never to leave him again. The offering was wrung from him at enormous cost, for by nature " he never had any particular devotion to the poor, nay, rather the opposite." The incident was one to which—like his period of slavery—he never referred.

He continued his work at the hospital, which was, after all, wholly concerned with the very poor. Then this work was increased, as he was appointed almoner and chaplain to *la Reine Margot*, that one-time Queen of France. Like many other great sinners, she was also a great giver, and it was her delight, now that she was old and fat and unattractive, to help all who were in trouble. She had several almoners—priests chosen by her to administer her *largesse*—and possibly through one of these she and Vincent became known to one another.

The appointment was a godsend to Vincent, since the money from it helped him to reduce his strangling debts. Then fortune smiled on him again when he was made curé of the church at Clichy, then a small country town on the outskirts of Paris. Very quickly he grew to love each one of the six hundred souls who composed his parish, and they as quickly grew to love him. They found in him a man of experience and intelligence, and one who was well educated. Had he not taken several degrees! He was also an excellent teacher, besides being something of a preacher.

His preaching, indeed, was a revelation to his hearers, who would listen spell-bound to his sermons. They were not only easy to understand, but were also so interesting that all looked forward to going to church just to listen to them alone. A certain slight difficulty of speech hampered him somewhat, but this was atoned for by his gift for drama and for mimicry. Often in the pulpit he would carry on conversations between himself and some imaginary person, which would hold his hearers entranced, and he never minded if his sallies sometimes provoked laughter.

His dignity he never lost at any time, and although he came of peasant stock—and very fine stock it was—there was nothing about him to suggest the peasant. In bearing he was quiet, grave, even majestic. Tall and dark, he wore at this time the slight moustache and closely cropped beard, characteristic of most French clergy of the day. His complexion was brown, his face was very strong, but all who came in contact with him were struck most forcibly by his eyes—"dark, deep-set, twinkling with mischief, irony and humour."

His life at Clichy was that of an ordinary parish priest. Year after year passed with nothing spectacular to mark them. The church was so much out of repair that it was in process of falling down when he first took over the charge of it; but he, being in touch with people of wealth in Paris, soon managed to raise money to restore it. He was regarded by his people as their closest friend; they came to him in all their difficulties. "How are you getting on, Monsieur?" the Cardinal of Paris asked him one day. "Monseigneur," he replied, "I am more happy than I can express. Neither his Holiness himself, nor you, Monseigneur, could be so happy as I am."

Then in a moment all this happiness was taken from him, as de Bérulle, still his director and confessor, counselled him to give up this work which he was doing, and to undertake instead a task which to one of his temperament could hardly have been more distasteful. He was to leave his church and his people, and laying aside his freedom and so many of the functions of his priesthood, he was to enter the house of a great nobleman, there to be tutor to this nobleman's two most unattractive little boys. What fate could have been more dreary? What advice could have been more unexpected? And what about his vow which he had made to serve the poor? De Bérulle knew as much about it as Vincent did, and yet his counsel remained unwavering. So Vincent, feeling that such counsel must constitute for him the will of God—which had become by then the only thing that mattered to him—accepted it and did so without question.

"To leave all things without the hope of possessing anything," he was to say years after, with memory perhaps alive in him of the bitter struggle which this change in his life must of necessity have brought him; "without knowing what is going to happen to you, without any other assurance than confidence in God—is not that the life of Jesus Christ? Is there anything greater, anything more noble?" "Perfection," he said on another occasion, "is it not a loving, sweet union of the will with that of God?"

The name of the man into whose employment he was to be taken was Monseigneur Phillipe de Gondi, Comte de Joigny and General of the Galleys. He was the head of one of France's most wealthy families and was the owner of vast estates. He was good and kindly and his wife, whom he adored, was beautiful and devout. But his boys were described by an aunt who knew them as " veritable little demons."

CHAPTER III

The Gilded Cage

VINCENT remained for twelve years in the service of the de Gondis, and it is safe to say that those years were to him the longest of his life. Frustration, such as he had never known before, marked them, even though from the worldly point of view they gave him much—security, a life of ease, if he chose to make it so, even of luxury. Great affection was poured upon him. But in return he sacrificed everything that he held most dear—not only his work at Clichy and the many contacts in Paris which his friendship with de Bérulle brought him, but besides, and above all, his liberty and the whole background of his priestly life. With the de Gondis his position was that of a superior servant; their lovely châteaux in the country, their palace in Paris constituting for him only a gilded cage. And reading the history of this time, we are surprised at first by de Bérulle's counsel, which was in fact to prove most wise. For Vincent, so far as anyone can judge, would have remained unknown to history, few, if any, of his works achieved, if he had not been willing to assume the yoke which de Bérulle indicated to him.

De Bérulle, knowing the great temporal power of the de Gondis, and aware, as few others were, of Vincent's equally great spiritual power and other powers too, may have glimpsed something of the value their friendship might be to him. It would in any case have been part of his spirituality to be certain that the very costliness of the step towards which he was directing Vincent was likely to assure results of peculiar richness. Monsieur and Madame de Gondi also were close friends of his, and they had brought much pressure to bear on him to find a suitable tutor for their sons. The tutor must be a priest, and a priest, moreover, who would share their home, and not every priest in Paris would have been capable of doing this. " The great ranked their priests amongst their inferior servants," a contemporary writes, " and their society was slighted, for they were examples of boorishness and did not even know what cleanliness was." Vincent, with his innate refinement and delicacy of spirit, would have offered startling contrast to such a type, and there was no doubt of his teaching powers. His capacity in this regard had been shown both at Dax and at Toulouse. He was thus in every way an ideal person for a post which was most difficult to fill.

It was during the autumn of 1613 that he left Clichy and with heavy heart travelled towards Montmirail, another small place near Paris where one of the de Gondis' many châteaux stood. It was a large building, surrounded by gardens and filled with numerous servants. Great riches and great luxury pervaded it, yet the two owners of it were quite simple in the midst of their surrounding state, and both were attracted from the first to the young priest whom de Bérulle had found for them. A room of his own was given to him, hidden somewhere in the vast pile, and the moments when he could be alone there were what made his new life bearable to him. He used the room, we are told, as a monk would use his cell. There he would find peace from the turbulent, excited, chattering world pressing so closely on him.

He had at first only one pupil—the de Gondis' eldest son, a boy of eleven years old ; the next in age was still too small for lessons. Another boy had been born just before Vincent's arrival. His tutorial work was thus not arduous ; but he was presently given the spiritual care and instruction of his patron's servants, after which—as his powers were realised—his labours were further extended to the tenants living on the de Gondi estates.

His gilded cage was thus made more bearable, but it remained a cage, and his loneliness increased. No point of contact existed between him and the people who composed the de Gondis' world. Things which interested him they would know nothing about. He must share to the uttermost their lives, while there was none to take any share in his. The prattle of exotic people, many of them quite unintelligent, absorbed hours of his time, which he could have filled so differently. It was small wonder then that, as weeks and months and soon years passed by, he should often look forth with yearning to the world which he had left. Depression had always been a recognised enemy with him, and it assailed him frequently now, though little sign of it was ever visible to those who lived closest to him. They saw him for the most part as an inconspicuous young priest, though one possessed already of a wisdom which at times was startling, and also of spiritual powers which were unusual.

These last his patrons were quick to note, and after about a year of close contact with him Madame de Gondi approached him with the request that he should become her confessor. He refused at once, his reasons for such a refusal being quite easy to understand. For she was excessively devout, rather stupid and so scrupulous that to be her director would necessitate not only infinite patience, but an immense expenditure of time. Her pictured face shows kindliness but great obstinacy. Most priests are acquainted with her type, and it is not one whose guidance they ever covet.

Vincent remained adamant in his refusal of her request; she remained equally adamant in her determination that he should grant it, and eventually she won. She applied to de Bérulle to bring pressure to bear on him, and de Bérulle having done so, Vincent yielded and she was at peace. " He had much to endure," we learn, " from her tendency to scrupulosity. She wished to have him by her side both in the house and on her travels. When he was absent, she feared lest an accident or an illness had deprived her of him and kept urging him to return." Vincent with his usual shrewdness saw all this as an exaggerated self-love and sought to combat it by giving her work amongst her own dependents. She responded. She had a germ of real religion in her, and soon she was working for the poor on her estates as eagerly and almost as wisely as Vincent himself.

They worked together thus for some two years when, one January evening of 1617, a curious incident occurred. The family was staying at one of their châteaux near Amiens when a message came for Vincent to go to a man who was dying in the neighbouring village. The man was good-living and respected by all around, but now that he was near to death, he was haunted by the weight and magnitude of the evil he had done. He wanted to see Vincent and the latter went to him at once, heard his general confession and left him completely at peace. The man was alive the next morning when Vincent went once more to see him, accompanied now by Madame de Gondi. "Ah, Madame," the sick man said to her with shining eyes, " I should have been damned indeed, if I had not made a general confession, on account of the many great sins I have committed and which I had never dared confess before." The words conveyed, though quite unwittingly, the most disturbing state of ignorance in which he, and doubtless many others were living.

" O Monsieur Vincent, listen to that! " cried Madame de Gondi. "Just think of what we have heard! O sir, how many souls are perishing! What is the remedy for such a state of affairs ? " The remedy was applied quite simply by Vincent the following Sunday in the shape of a sermon, which set forth so clearly the nature and value of confession and of general confession in particular that his confessional was at once besieged. So many came to it, indeed, that he was obliged to call in the help of neighbouring priests.

The incident and its sequel opened the eyes of Vincent and of Madame de Gondi, not only to the prevailing ignorance of the Catholic faith in the countryside, but also to the extraordinary response which the people were ready to give to that faith when it was presented to them in a way that they could understand. Here, all unknown to anyone, was the germ from which Vincent's future Company of Mission Priests was to spring. For Vincent continued to ponder on these recent happenings, and the more he did so, the more he realised that they had shown him work which needed to be done and for which he was pre-eminently fitted. If only he were free to do it! The bars of his prison-house pressed then more closely than ever before. No need now to recall his vow of service to the poor! It was the one service of all others that he was wanting to make his own.

Winter passed, spring came. Vincent could not settle down and at last he approached de Bérulle with a veritable *cri de cœur* for freedom. " Is it fitting," he asked, " that I should spend the greater part of my time within the narrow circle of a single family giving lessons to two or three children, when so many souls in these country villages are endangering their eternal salvation for lack of something I could give them?" So he wrote, then went on to stress all the advantages which his departure from the de Gondis would bring about. He himself would be protected from the temptation to vanity to which their esteem and respect exposed him. He would be cut off also from the excessive attachment of Madame de Gondi for him, while it would give her children a chance of having a tutor endowed with qualities which he did not believe that he possessed.

The care with which he searched out these various reasons can be imagined, also the eagerness with which he waited for a reply from the man in whose wisdom he trusted so completely. The reply was swift in coming.

Vincent's problem had arrived at a most opportune moment, for de Bérulle, who had lately established a company of priests known as the Oratorians, had received almost simultaneously a request from one of them, who was Superior of a house at Lyons, for a zealous young priest to go at once to a country parish named Châtillon not far from the city. Many abuses were known to be prevailing in the place where much work was waiting to be done. Vincent would be eminently suited for such a post, and de Bérulle advised his acceptance of it.

The de Gondis happened to be away while all this was happening, and Vincent, like the escaping prisoner that he was, hurried off without a moment's delay. He left only a message for his patrons which said that he was " making a little journey." He did not add that he hoped it was a journey from which there would be no return. It was July and there were few happier people in the whole of France than he as he posted quickly southward.

Difficulties met him immediately he arrived at Châtillon, but they were of a kind to interest and to stimulate him. Nevertheless, the work awaiting him was so heavy that he had to ask for another priest to help him, and on the latter's arrival the two started at once to live a conventual life, saying the Office together, and rising each day at five o'clock. Vincent quickly learned the *patois* of the district. He taught and preached and visited. "Châtillon," we are told, "was transformed in four months." The work, thus successfully begun, resembled very closely all that he had done at Clichy, until all at once it was enlarged, as a result of a little incident, not unlike that which had occurred the previous January near Amiens.

Vincent was in his vestry one burning September morning vesting to say Mass when a messenger appeared to tell him of a family, living about three miles away, who were all of them so ill that none could raise a finger to help the other. "They were in such dire straits," Vincent recounts himself, "as cannot be expressed. I was moved to the depths of my heart and did not fail to speak feelingly of them during the sermon. And God, touching the hearts of those who were listening, caused them all to be moved with compassion also for the poor afflicted people."

His words must have, indeed, been moving, for in spite of the heat, a meeting was held that afternoon "at the house of a good lady in the town," and it was resolved to bring help at once to this most distressful family. Little bands of warm-hearted people started off immediately, and when Vincent himself followed them after Vespers, he found what he describes as "a regular procession on the roads." Generosity so lavish exceeded the needs of just one family, but the good will behind it was so wonderful that it needed to be made use of, and this Vincent proceeded to do. He called a meeting a few days after of the well-to-do women of his parish and they— banding themselves together by some simple rules to help all those who were in distress of any kind—became thus the first of Vincent de Paul's famous Confraternities of Charity. It was a simple beginning to one of the greatest reforms which even he ever brought about.

The summer thus passed, autumn was soon flaming in the fields and vineyards, and Vincent was for the second time in his life superlatively happy. But what of the de Gondis? They were a memory which he doubtless thrust away from him each time he was assailed by it, though he had quieted his conscience somewhat by writing a letter to Monsieur de Gondi soon after his arrival at Châtillon, explaining that he had decided to give up the work for which the General of the Galleys had engaged him. A different tutor, he considered, was needed for the General's sons, and he hoped optimistically that the General would think so too.

Posts took a long time to arrive at their destinations in those days, a fact which was in Vincent's favour, and Monsieur de Gondi being still away from home, Vincent's letter was delayed in reaching him. His reaction on receiving it was one of despair and he at once sat down to share with his wife the dire news.

" I am in despair," he writes, " and I beg you to do everything that is in your power not to lose him." He then suggests the possible intervention of his own sister, but adds—" I think, however, that no one will be more powerful than Monsieur de Bérulle. Tell him that even if it were true that Monsieur Vincent could not teach youths, he could have a man under him. But no matter what happens, I passionately desire his return to my house in which he can live just as he pleases."

This letter, with that from Vincent enclosed, did not reach Madame de Gondi until the middle of September and their effect upon her was overwhelming. She wept day and night, she refused to eat and ceased her tears only to write reproaches to Vincent and to de Bérulle. Her letters, which are most revealing documents, are not without a touch of sadness, since they show how little either her efforts, or Vincent's direction had made towards the selflessness which she so deeply needed. One can picture with what shrinking Vincent read them.

" I should not suffer so much," she wrote to him, " if it were only for a little time that I should lose you, but when I reflect on all the occasions in which I shall need to be assisted by guidance and advice, both in life and death, my sorrows are renewed. . . . If after all this, you still refuse to return, I will charge you before God for all that may befall me, and for all the good that I shall fail to accomplish through being left unaided. . . . My soul also should be assisted at the hour of death. Remember the last illness which I had. . . . I shall soon probably be in a worse state." Thus to Vincent, and then to de Bérulle. " I bring no accusation against him ; far from it. Yet in truth his flight is most strange. I confess I can make nothing of it. He knows the need I have of his

guidance and the matters I have to confide to him; the bodily
and mental sufferings I have endured through lack of assistance; the good I wish to do in my villages and that it is
impossible for me to carry out without his advice. In short,
I see my soul in a most pitiable state. You see with what
feelings of annoyance the General wrote to me. My children
are day by day wasting away, and the good he did in my home
and to the seven or eight thousand souls on my estates is gone
forever. What! Have not these souls been redeemed by the
precious blood of Our Lord as well as those in Bresse? Are
they not just as dear to Him? In truth, I know not what
Monsieur Vincent thinks of that. But it seems to me of such
importance that I will do everything in my power to get him
back."

She certainly did. She demanded prayers from bishops,
priests and members of communities and finally despatched
her husband's secretary to Châtillon with a bundle of letters
so enormous that he must have staggered beneath its weight.
The letters were from " the Bishop of Paris, from Monsieur
de Bérulle, from Madame de Gondi herself, her children,
her nearest relations, the chief officers of her household,
doctors of divinity, members of religious communities, besides
many persons of rank and piety." Was ever so gratifying a
post received by anyone with so much sorrow and sinking
of heart!

There was only one amongst all the letters which really
counted with Vincent, that from Monsieur de Bérulle, and
de Bérulle gave no counsel in it. He just described Madame
de Gondi's condition of distress and left it to Vincent to decide
what he should do. Vincent was bewildered, for added to
all these written supplications were the unceasing verbal
petitions of Monsieur de Gondi's secretary, these last possibly
not wholly selfless. For what could be more torturing than
life under the de Gondi roof with Madame de Gondi in her
present state? Let Vincent return and quiet her at any
price. But Vincent was always slow in making decisions,
and now he sat down and wrote to the Superior of the
Oratorians in Lyons, whom he regarded as his Superior too.
The latter counselled him to return to Paris and talk the whole
matter over with Monsieur de Bérulle and others there. And

as Vincent read that letter, he must have known his doom was sealed. For Madame de Gondi was in Paris and there could be no escaping her. So he preached a farewell sermon in the church which he had already grown to love, a sermon which we are told, was received by the congregation with stupefaction and with sobs. The day on which he finally left the little town was regarded by its inhabitants as one of mourning. People looked after the cart in which he drove away until it was out of sight, then returned desolate and sorrowful to their homes.

Vincent reached Paris on December 23, and on the following day he had an interview with Madame de Gondi, who received him, Vincent's first biographer tells us, " as if he were an angel from heaven." And now that she knew she could hope with a measure of certainty that he would return to her, she was prepared to lavish generosity upon him. He should be no longer tutor to her children, so she said, but chaplain of her household and estates, and those estates with their eight thousand souls should be his parish over which he might have command to establish Confraternities of Charity, to organise missions, or to do anything else he liked. She both gave and bequeathed money to establish a band of mission priests to work under him. There were no limits to her lavishness. She would give him everything, except one thing—his freedom.

Vincent, faced by such a situation, could do nothing but accept it and he wrote out in January his resignation of Châtillon. The doors of his gilded cage were once more closed upon him, but this time they were closed irrevocably, so he thought, for he had given Madame de Gondi a solemn promise that he would remain in her service for so long as she was alive ; he must never try to escape again. He was thirty-seven and she was younger by several years. The life for which he wished so much was evidently not for him. So with the first piercing sorrow of his wrench from Châtillon overcome, he settled down once more with this family who loved him far too well. His lot was better than it had been formerly, for he was delivered from the bondage of the school-room and he had been given more opportunities for work outside. He resolved to make the best of these in the years that stretched ahead, and most assuredly he succeeded.

CHAPTER IV

The Opening of the Cage

HIS life now changed considerably; Madame de Gondi being, indeed, true to all the promises she had made. Greater freedom was henceforth his, while his patrons endeavoured to curb their demands upon him. His actual position, however, remained much as before. He was still the de Gondis' servant, liable to be summoned by them at any moment from whatever he might be doing. His headquarters were always at one or other of their châteaux. An ordered priestly life was still denied him. But his resolve to make the best of what had been given him held good, and when he returned to Montmirail during that January of 1618, he set off immediately upon a mission which he had already planned. And he did not set forth alone; some other priests joined him, for he was beginning now to be well known. The story of his escape from his patrons and his forced return to them had created a certain mild sensation in the capital, where more and more people were beginning to wonder about him. Many of the great of Paris knew him already, having met him on their visits to the de Gondis. Now, however, they would see him less often, his work taking him increasingly far afield.

His five months at Châtillon had taught him much, and at the first town where he went to stay on this first mission, he started immediately one of those Confraternities of Charity which he had found already of so much value. Its establishment, like that at Châtillon, was very practical, the aim of its work being, as he explained to another little company of well-to-do ladies, to give corporal and spiritual help to the poor around. Those who were sick were to be visited in their own homes and provided with medicine and food and clothing, while spiritual aid was to be given wherever possible. Money for all this was to be obtained by begging, by collections in

22

churches, by appeals to the very rich around and by appeals also to municipal authorities. All members elected to the Confraternity were to be under the authority of their curé, and all work was to be done " lovingly " and for the sake of Jesus Christ alone. The idea made a swift appeal, and Confraternities sprang up almost automatically wherever Vincent went.

A wave of compassion was just beginning to sweep over France, bringing with it an awakening to the terrible lot of many of the peasantry, ground down, as they were, by merciless taxation. Deaths from cold, hunger, or neglect were ordinary events. Vincent, already aware of these conditions, became even more so as he travelled over one district after another of northern France. Yet he, practical peasant that he was, refused to be carried away by them. He eyed them with sympathy, yet with shrewdness too, and incidents which would have doubtless shocked the ignorant town-dweller, left him questioning. Genuine misery he was ready to alleviate at any price, but for the professional beggar, or those eager to make parade of their afflictions he had small sympathy.

He came across a flagrant case of the professional beggar and the menace he can be, in the course of these early travels. The experience was unexpected and shows how swiftly he could act when the occasion demanded swiftness. Usually his way led him through small villages, but on this occasion he had to pass through a large-sized town, that of Mâcon, and there he was shocked by the numbers of beggars infesting streets and churches. All of them, he noticed, were of an abandoned type, while many were obviously able-bodied. The idea of staying in the town had not occurred to him, but now in a moment he decided to ask the hospitality of some Oratorian Fathers living on the outskirts. They were delighted to give it to him and supplied him with any help they could, as he proceeded to draw up a register of all the indigent persons of the town, in number about three hundred. He suggested then that help should be given them only on fixed days, unless they were really too ill to work. Each Sunday they were to assemble at the parish church for Mass, and a Confraternity of Charity, consisting of men as well as women, was to look after them.

The simplicity of the scheme set forth is as startling as its success. Vincent remained at Mâcon a bare three days, yet in that time he managed to work a transformation in its previous beggar-infested streets ; the town wore a different air. And the Oratorians, looking on, were as much impressed by this as by Vincent's capacity for making others work. " Soon everybody, small and great, were eager to help in every way."

Here was specifically social work, while work of a more spiritual order was Vincent's real aim. He saw his missions as of immeasurably greater importance than anything he might do on a more philanthropic level. It was the souls of these poor people which he and his fellow-priests were anxious above all else to save, and many, indeed, came to the Christ he preached in the course of his long travels. His vivid, dramatic sermons won them, but even more the love for them with which he was so obviously filled, and which owed its power to his own over-mastering love for the Christ of whom he told them. These winter months were thrilling months indeed. What mattered the cold, or the following great heat!

But his time was not only spent in this country work he loved. Paris was often visited by the de Gondis and his presence with them there was always perforce demanded. All pastoral work must then be laid aside, and the whole background of his life exchanged for another which offered sharpest contrast. The Paris house, which the de Gondis owned, situated in the most fashionable quarter of the city, would be filled with crowds of people. Balls, operas, concerts, visits to the royal palace of the Louvre would be the order of the day. Bustle, movement, noise, confusion would reign unceasingly, in all of which things Vincent could have no real part. He would be glad, indeed, to escape from them to the quiet of de Bérulle's Oratorian house, or to some nearby church.

Then, on one of these early visits to Paris, a very happy experience was his, as he came into contact for the first time with Francis de Sales, Bishop of Geneva, a close friend of de Bérulle, and as great a spiritual force. He and Vincent were at once attracted to each other. Francis was the elder of the two, but the same gentleness and penetration and humour, the same love of Christ marked both, and they talked for long hours together. Francis, highly educated, member of a Savoyard family, so old that its origins were lost in antiquity, and as much at home amongst kings and courtiers as the de Gondis, felt no barriers separating him from Vincent and Vincent felt none either. Later Vincent was to describe him as the most completely Christ-like man whom he had ever met. A friendship thus begun, continued to grow ever deeper as years passed by.

Vincent could be accounted now as living at the very heart of French life. For here in Paris he was aware of everything of moment happening in the capital, while his knowledge was considerable of provincial and country life of which so few dwellers in towns knew anything at all. Then his knowledge was further deepened by work which he could not have touched except through the influence of Monsieur de Gondi. " General of the Galleys " was one of the latter's many high-sounding titles, and through the power which that title brought him, Vincent was enabled to penetrate places which would otherwise have been closed to him, and to touch suffering—and to alleviate it—which he would not otherwise have known existed.

The Conciergerie, then and for so many years after, the great prison of Paris, housed within its walls many prisoners condemned to the galleys. These awaited their removal to Marseilles from which port they would be transferred to the king's ships, in whose terrible holds their lives would largely be lived. For the first time now Vincent entered this prison and found in it conditions which horrified him. Even the poorest room or hovel he had ever entered before was " as a palace " compared with the dark, damp, airless, vermin-ridden holds in which these men lay chained for weeks and sometimes months on end. They lay there forgotten by everybody. Neither spiritual nor material help was ever given them ; only jailers ever visited them. "And their sufferings," we learn without surprise, " instead of opening their hearts and making them repent, filled them only with revolt and blasphemy."

Vincent, stirred more deeply than he had ever been before, was not long in communicating to others what he had seen. And as a result of his words, the treatment of these men was to a certain extent improved, while the Cardinal of Paris was presently moved to enjoin his clergy to recommend these unfortunate men to the charity of the faithful.

Meanwhile, Vincent was their constant visitor, bringing to them the same deep, tender love which had won so many hearts already. Such work could not be hidden. He started off to do it from the de Gondis' house, and returned thither when his task was done. And as he was questioned by those who had watched him going and returning, he found amongst them some who were genuinely interested in all he had to say. Drama always invests a prison to those who are outside it, and dramatic, indeed, was the response which Vincent was gaining from these seemingly lost souls. " Eyes," we are told, " which had never been known to weep before, shed tears with which his hands were bathed." Soon absolution and Communion were demanded from men who had been considered before to be beyond redemption.

Then Vincent asked to be allowed to go to Marseilles, where he found conditions more terrible than those in Paris. Again he sought to alleviate them and was helped to do so by his appointment as Royal Almoner of the Galleys. This position, however, brought him only spiritual power ; there was little he could do to lessen on a material level the merciless treatment of the men. Sometimes they were taken from Paris to Bordeaux—chained together by their necks and leaving a blood-stained path behind them—and it was at Bordeaux that he once held a mission for them, and from thence went to his old home, a visit to which he looked forward with mingled feelings of pleasure and apprehension.

Some fifteen years had passed since he had crossed the threshold of the little farmstead of his youth, and he feared, as he approached it, that love for it might lay too strong a hold on him. It was in its neighbourhood that he had thought to end his days during that period in Paris when he had been so miserable, and still the thought of doing so beckoned to him. He was essentially a country-man, and here would be peace and certain refuge from the storm and stress of his increasingly busy life. He was at heart a contemplative—as one is so apt to forget when faced by the history of his immense activity—and, to the contemplative, solitude and silence are as a breath of heaven. A little benefice here would bring that heaven to him. But the temptation was set aside, and his visit did not last for long. Indeed, a certain constraint marked it on both sides, which is not surprising when it is remembered that he was something of a stranger to his mother and his several brothers and sisters. They remembered a youthful priest, ambitious, keen on teaching, more than a trifle worldly. Here was a man of nearly forty, quiet, austere, who slept on a straw mattress, who mixed water plentifully with his wine, and who walked barefoot to a pilgrimage chapel near. His visit also brought them a certain disappointment—as we know from an account of it left behind by Vincent—for they were expecting much from it in the way of gifts and worldly advancement. Was not Vincent a friend of the richest in the land? But he gave them nothing, explaining that he had nothing to give, since any money which might seem to be his belonged not to him but to God and to God's poor.

The action was so hard that it caused Vincent himself disquiet. Memory of it " hung a continual weight upon his spirit" for many months to come, as he wondered if he had been right to behave in such a fashion towards relations, who had been in the past so generous to him. Logically, his conduct was correct. He had repaid long since the money that he owed them, and they were not poor, as he knew poverty. His decision rankled, nevertheless, and, perhaps, shocks those who read of it today. It underlines, however, an aspect of his character which was a very strong one—an austerity and severity, together with a detachment, amounting at times to harshness. Later it was to form the basis of his direction of the many souls who came to him for guidance. They must never depend on him, he taught them, neither on his gifts, nor his words, nor yet his sympathy. For God, and not he, was to be their sole and only strength and refuge. So now his continual scruples regarding his recent treatment of his family were silenced at last only as he commended them to God with that intensity of prayer of which he was a master. An essential tenderness is revealed, however, in the very fact that the incident should have given him the disquiet which it did.

The year 1622 brought with it a great sorrow in the sudden death of Francis de Sales. Few mourned him more deeply

than did Vincent. All that contemplative side of his nature
Francis had understood. He thought so highly of it, indeed,
that some time previously he had asked Vincent to take over
the direction of the Paris house of a convent of contemplative
nuns which he had founded. It was the Order of the Visitation
and was ruled by Jeanne de Chantal, later to be Sainte Chantal.
Now on his death Vincent became Superior of the whole
Order, a difficult task, but one which Francis willed that he
should undertake.

Vincent lived with the de Gondis for nearly seven years
after his return from Châtillon, years which bore much fruit
and which must have been marked often by great happiness
for him. Depression, nevertheless, assailed him often, though
blame for it he attributed always to himself and not to his
employers. He mostly managed to hide what he was feeling,
but he could not always succeed, and once Madame de Gondi
spoke to him of his apparent unhappiness. Was it her fault,
she questioned. The question startled him. " I addressed
myself then at once to God," he notes, " and prayed that my
hard, repulsive nature might be changed into one of gentleness
and kindness, and by God's grace I have been enabled to
conquer a little my dark humours."

Such conquest must have been made the easier when
Madame de Gondi, during the early spring of 1625, presented
him with a house in Paris, to be the headquarters of a company
of mission priests of his own choosing. The house was very
old and in a state of dilapidation, but Vincent loved it from
the first and threw himself whole-heartedly into arrangements
for its habitation.

It was the Collège des Bons Enfants and, dating from the
thirteenth century, was well known in Paris. Intended originally as a hostel for students, it had remained so always and
housed still about eight young men, all of whom Vincent
allowed to remain on beneath its very leaky roof. The building,
although large and spacious, was not capacious. Long,
draughty corridors and passages occupied much valuable
space. Cracked windows were everywhere. There was a
general air of decay and desolation. Yet the house was a
religious one and Vincent, as head of it, could do what he
liked with it.

He bound himself, at the same time that it became his, to form within a year an association of at least six priests, who should devote themselves unreservedly to " the salvation of poor country folk," the men to be all of " proved doctrine, piety and learning." Vincent was to be their Superior, though a Superior, who was debarred from living amongst his sons. The de Gondis made it abundantly clear that he was to " continue to reside in their house, rendering them the same spiritual assistance which he had always given them."

Whether a community separated thus from its founder and superior would have survived is questionable. But Vincent, perhaps, did not think of this as he signed on April 17, 1625, a contract, which may still be seen, by which house and community became his own. And he was searching about for priests with which to fill the house when all at once something quite unforeseen occurred. Madame de Gondi fell ill. She often was ill, but from this illness it was destined she should not recover. Spring passed and her weakness increased, then in June she died, with Vincent at her side, as she had always wished he would be.

No event could have been more unexpected by Vincent. He had made complete surrender of his freedom, and now all in a moment freedom was to be his. Madame de Gondi, it is true, had left in her will a wish that he should remain with her family always. But Monsieur de Gondi refused to sanction such a sacrifice, and before the end of the year Vincent had left the service of this family which had exacted much from him, but from which he had gained almost as much as he had given. He started at once to live in his new house, and thus at the age of forty-four found himself his own master at last. For the third time in his life he was superlatively happy.

CHAPTER V

Saint Lazare

HE set forth on the first of his missions from his new home during the December of this year, and was accompanied then by two other priests, all three being bound together by a simple rule of his devising. Upon this day his famous Congregation of Mission Priests may be said to have been born. Years afterwards he thus described the work which was now begun. " The three of us used to go and give missions, passing from village to village. When we set out, we would give the key of our house to one of our neighbours or beg him to go and sleep in it at night. I had only one sermon myself, and I used to twist and turn it in a thousand ways ; it was on the fear of God. That is how we proceeded, and yet God was effecting what He had foreseen from all eternity. He gave some blessings to our labours and some good ecclesiastics, seeing this, joined us." Slowly and quietly they did so, until a moment came when Vincent was ruling quite a substantial number.

Each mission was carefully planned and none took place between June 24 and November 1, when the harvest was gathered in. The curés of the parishes, where the missions were to be held, were approached always with greatest courtesy, while it was made clear to them that they would be involved in no expense connected with the mission. One of Vincent's maxims was that everything should be done in accordance with their wishes and ideas. " When we begin or conclude a mission, we ask for their blessing in a spirit of submission."

One of the missioners arrived always on the Sunday before the mission was to begin, and preached then two sermons— the first on the value of the mission itself and the second on the value of general confession. The rest of the missioners followed shortly after and were given lodgings for which they paid, or else an empty house, which they fitted up with furniture of their own transported on "a little cart." Thus established—and very often accompanied by a lay brother to look after their material wants—they could work together and live their religious life together. They rose each morning at four o'clock, and from then until nine o'clock or even ten at night, their days were fully occupied. They preached, catechised, visited the sick, established Confraternities of Charity, reconciled those who were at enmity, instructed school-masters and school-mistresses, and lived at the same time their own strict lives of prayer. They said Mass each day and recited the Offices. They had special times for general and particular examination of conscience, besides time for mental prayer.

And people crowded to hear them. Most of those who came possessed some sort of rudiments of faith, and these men who addressed them were well trained, each of them being gifted with that power, which was Vincent's too, of being able to make every subject interesting of which they spoke. " How do we find that the Apostles preached ? " Vincent wrote once. " In friendly fashion, familiarly and simply. Now look at our manner of preaching : in homely language, naturally, in all simplicity. To preach as the Apostles did, we must be simple and use ordinary words, so that everyone may be able to understand and profit. It was thus that the disciples and Apostles preached ; it was thus also that Jesus Christ preached."

The importance of the catechism Vincent never tired of emphasising. He and his missioners would walk about amongst the children, talking to them very gently, instructing them very carefully. Sometimes it would happen that one or other of the eager listeners would be found " sufficiently instructed to approach the Holy Table for the first time." Then a sermon would be preached about the event. " It is one of the best means we have," wrote Vincent, " to touch older people whose hearts are hard and obstinate. They will often allow themselves to be won by the devotion of the children and by the care that is taken of them."

The first sermon was always preached very early in the morning before men and women went out to work in the fields. Another was preached in the evening, or at whatever time best suited the people. The missions lasted mostly for quite lengthy periods—seldom for less than fifteen days, while they sometimes stretched over a space of two months, " according to the size and importance of the parish and the disposition of the inhabitants." They came to an end when it was calculated that a general confession had been made by all. Missionary work was interrupted every week for one day, and at the end of each mission the missioners themselves took a rest of several days, which they used as " a period of recollection." A further period of twelve days' quiet followed when they made preparations for the succeeding mission.

As the Congregation of the Missions grew, Vincent realised more and more the importance of the " vacation " of his sons, those months of late summer and autumn, spent always at the Collège des Bons Enfants, when there was no specific work to do. All must revise their theology then, studies must be deepened, and sermons read to members of the Congregation, who would closely criticise them. Training in matters of controversy was also undertaken. Nothing, indeed, was left undone to perfect these men in work which was to Vincent of such infinite importance.

For some seven years he continued to live thus happily at the Collège des Bons Enfants with his steadily growing band of followers. Their numbers were presently large enough for them to receive legal status, and Papal approval followed later. Men who were real scholars were now to be found in the Congregation, and the Collège des Bons Enfants was being stretched almost to capacity to find room to house them all.

Vincent was content, indeed, and asked no more than just to be allowed to go on year after year doing this work he loved so well. He always disliked change, and never wanted to increase his influence. The large part he was soon to play in the reform of so many abuses of the day was thrust upon him ; nothing of it was of his own choosing. But it was small wonder that his help should be constantly asked, since it was he, who seeing so often the evil, saw equally—with his clear vision—the remedy.

His work amongst these " poor country-folk " had opened his eyes, as we have seen, to many prevailing evils, and some he had been able to remedy. But that which was the greatest of them all baffled him—the condition of the priesthood. He

had known that the priesthood had sunk low, but the actual
depths of its degradation were hidden from him until now,
as his journeys led him further and further from Paris.

The wars of religion had much to do with it. Churches,
wrecked by troops, had in many cases remained unbuilt, or
if they were still in use, they were in a ruined state " without
books, or vestments, or even tabernacles." The last were
often made of copper, and the Host within them would be
sometimes mildewed, or even eaten by mice, so little did
priestly guardians care. In 1628 a Bishop wrote of his diocese
that it contained " nearly seven thousand priests, who are
drunkards or immoral, and without vocation of any sort."
Many did not know the words of absolution. " The Church
has no enemies so dangerous as her priests," wrote Vincent.
" It is due to the priests that the heretics have flourished, that
vice has gained its mastery, and that ignorance is so prevalent
amongst the people."

And seeing all this, Vincent said little, but he pondered
deeply. Much was being done in Paris for the reform of the
clergy, but nothing was being done for those in the country.
And what could be done for them ? Vincent, still watching,
still pondering, came to the slow conclusion that there was,
indeed, no remedy at all for conditions such as he had seen.
The evil had gone too far. Reform could be brought about
only through a concentration on those who were preparing
for the priesthood, young men, who should be taught and
trained and moulded until they really were fitting instruments
for the high estate which would be theirs. Then, having thus
seen the evil, and what he considered to be its remedy, he
explained both to a certain Bishop of Beauvais, a friend of his
and a man of some influence.

" There is no use thinking," he said to him, " that we
can bring back to the path of duty priests who have grown old
in the habits of vice ; that would be sure to meet with a check.
It is far better to apply a remedy to the very source of the evil,
and in order to achieve this, we should do all in our power to
instruct those who wish to take Holy Orders in the duties of
their state, inspire them with the ecclesiastical spirit and
pitilessly refuse all who have not this spirit and who are
ignorant of their duties."

The suggestion awakened no apparent response from his listener, and Vincent just left the matter. Then, to his surprise as he was driving along in a coach one burning July day with this same Bishop, seemingly asleep beside him, the whole subject was referred to again. The Bishop suddenly opened his eyes and spoke.

" I believe," he said, " that I can see at last a short and efficacious means of preparing clerics for Holy Orders. I will take them into my house for several days, and there they shall give themselves up to devotional exercises and be instructed in their duties and functions."

" That idea, my Lord," Vincent replied, " has come straight to you from God. I can see no better means of bringing your clergy step by step back to the right way."

The Bishop acted quickly. A retreat for young ordinands was held in his palace before the coming September ordinations, and proved of so much value that the Archbishop of Paris immediately made plans for similar retreats to be held in the capital before each coming ordination. And searching round for some place in which to hold them, he decided that none could be better than the Collège des Bons Enfants. It had a large chapel, large adjoining rooms and it was ruled and owned by men of tried sanctity and experience. Vincent gave his consent; but in doing so, made it clear that, while he was extending to these young men the hospitality of his house, he was doing no more. Neither he nor his sons would play any part in the matter of the retreats, their work being confined exclusively to the preaching of missions in the country. And Vincent was so decisive that the Archbishop was forced to bow to his will.

The retreats became longer and larger. The Collège des Bons Enfants could hardly provide accommodation for the numbers who comprised them. The college also was becoming in other ways more and more a centre of religious activity in Paris. Vincent, therefore, should not have been so much surprised, as he certainly was, by an offer which was now made to him. It came from a certain Monsieur Adrian Le Bon, Prior of a small company of Augustinian monks who occupied the enormous building of Saint Lazare, situated in the very heart of Paris. This building, he suggested,

Vincent should share with him. The prospect appalled Vincent.

"Your proposal terrifies me," he said to the surprised Monsieur Le Bon, "for it seems to me to be so far above us that I should not even dare to think about it. We are poor priests; we live quite simply; our whole ambition is to be of service to poor country-folk. But we are deeply touched by your kindness and thank you very humbly for it."

"I hope," replied Le Bon, "that this is not your last word. Your Company will increase; you will be cooped up in this house you have now. The day is coming, indeed, when you will not know where to turn to provide accommodation for your community, and the possession of Saint Lazare then would relieve you of that worry. It is natural that you should want time to think the matter over, so I will come back again in another six months, and I hope by then that you will have arrived at a better understanding of your own interests."

But Vincent had arrived at no such understanding when Monsieur Le Bon returned, while the lengthy discussion which followed left him unmoved. And the proposition certainly was of a startling nature, the size of the building offered to him being alone enough to daunt him. It covered over a hundred acres of land, and boasted not only a Gothic church and cloisters, a chapel, a canon's house of residence and other buildings for monks, but also a prison, a windmill, a dove-cot, a granary, stables, cattle-sheds, a slaughter-house— besides many courtyards and extensive gardens and orchards. And the whole, it might be added, was in much the same state of dilapidation which Vincent had found at the Collège des Bons Enfants, for the foundation, like it, was very old.

Built originally for lepers, as its name suggests—Lazarus, who was raised from the dead, being its patron—its history had been marked by many vicissitudes, and it had been ful-filling little of late, chiefly because of the ineffectual rule of Monsieur Le Bon himself. His community had been reduced to only ten monks, though he was responsible also for the care of two lepers hidden somewhere in his huge building, besides some delinquent youths, who had been sent to him for care and protection. A lifelessness pervaded the whole structure, and it was small wonder that he should be so eager to share its governance with one of Vincent's vitality and strength. Equally it was small wonder that Vincent should hold back. And not only because he saw the building as a liability, but also, and even more, because of the anxiety of Le Bon to unite his own Order of Augustinians with Vincent's Company of Mission Priests.

To this Vincent could never give his consent. These Augustinians were known to be lax in the keeping of their Rule, which was in any case quite different from that which Vincent had devised for himself and his sons. Nothing that was good and much that was undesirable was likely to result to his Company from Monsieur Le Bon's proposal, while the position of two men, each holding the position of a Superior and living under the same roof, was fraught with difficulty. Altogether, the project had nothing to commend itself to Vincent, and he persisted in his refusal.

Le Bon was obstinate, however. He was determined, indeed, to bend Vincent to his will, and when he saw that his own words were of no avail, he approached others to plead his cause. A year passed, and Vincent began to weaken. He did so, however, only after all idea of the amalgamation of his Company and that of Le Bon's Order had been abandoned. He consented then to lay the question before a member of the Sorbonne, to whom it was obvious—as it was to many others—that it was Vincent's duty to accept the offer. Vincent stipulated then that, if he did so, his missioners must live completely cut off from Monsieur Le Bon's monks, having no intercourse with them of any kind. And to this Monsieur Le Bon agreed, and agreed also to Vincent becoming sole Superior of the house. He asked only that he might be allowed to retain his title of Prior, and his right of precedence in church and chapter and refectory, and that he might keep also the apartments which he had always occupied. To all these things Vincent readily agreed, and so at last on January 9, 1632, a contract between him and Monsieur Le Bon was signed. And on the same day of its signature Vincent and his missioners moved into their new home.

The move was momentous. The largest and most important ecclesiastical building in Paris now belonged to them, and they found themselves the centre of the religious work of the capital. Their power—which Vincent coveted so little—was immeasurably increased. The change had been thrust on Vincent. He had not wanted it, but having once accepted the burden which it involved, he assumed its responsibilities unquestioningly. He was nearly fifty-one when the change occurred. Only seven years had elapsed since Madame de Gondi's death.

CHAPTER VI

Louise de Marillac

SOME years before, when Vincent was still living with the de Gondis, he had come into contact with a woman, whose name will always be linked with his—Louise de Marillac, known also as Mademoiselle Le Gras. She, like the de Gondis, belonged to the great world of Paris, her father having held a high military appointment at court, while one of her uncles was Chancellor. She was married, her husband, Antoine Le Gras, being secretary to the Queen Regent, Marie de Medici. He, however, did not belong to the *haute noblesse*, so Louise became on her marriage to him Mademoiselle and not Madame.

She was twenty-three when she married, a shy, quiet girl, though one who was gifted with great charm and also an intelligence which was above the ordinary. Religion always meant much to her and she was something of a contemplative. Early caught into that wave of compassion which had begun to sweep over Paris, she discovered in herself, soon after her marriage, a gift for nursing. It became then her delight to slip away from her beautiful house and luxurious life to minister to the sick poor of Paris, washing them, dressing their wounds and shrinking neither from dirt, nor the extremity of suffering. After a little while others who belonged to her glittering world followed her example, and it was thus that she and they first came to hear of Vincent de Paul. She seems, however, to have made no personal contact with him until the beginning of the year 1625, the same year which saw later Madame de Gondi's death. She was advised then to ask him to become her confessor, a task which Vincent had no wish to undertake, since he saw in her just another wealthy, pious woman, who would only distract him from the work which he was longing to do. The future was veiled from him, and he could not see that much of that work would never have been accomplished but for her.

This year, so eventful to him, was equally so to her, for her husband died at the close of it, and she received the same freedom which had already been granted to Vincent. She gave up then her beautiful house in the most fashionable quarter of Paris and went to live instead in quite a small one on the other side of the river. She was nearer to the poor there, and to the Collège des Bons Enfants; she was also nearer to her only child, a schoolboy son whom she adored.

Her friendship with Vincent de Paul had by then deepened and developed. She was not, he found, the spoilt, worldly woman he had expected, but one of deep religion and of high intelligence; one, moreover, who was surprisingly selfless and eager to be trained. He welcomed, instead of deploring, the move which brought her so close to the Collège des Bons Enfants, and from there he often visited her. Soon a close companionship, which ranks amongst the most beautiful of religious history, was formed between the two. It became his delight to talk with her, and to share with her details of his missions and other interests. Her sympathy was unfailing, but when she asked him—as she frequently did—to enlarge the scope of her own life, he always refused. All unknown to her, he was trying and testing her, and also he was watching her most closely. He seldom praised her and he refused her always the close direction which her scrupulous and sometimes morbid nature craved.

Months passed, soon years passed. None of the gifts which she knew that she possessed were being used and a feeling of frustration—such as Vincent had experienced when he was living with the de Gondis—must often have been hers. But she curbed it, as she learned more and more deeply the lesson which Vincent was determined she should learn of selflessness and complete dependence upon God and on His will. Quite deliberately Vincent was fashioning an instrument, which he seems to have been well aware by then would soon be of the highest value to himself and to many others also.

It was only in 1629—four years after his first meeting with her—that he approached her at last with the request that she should do something for him. Would she, he asked, go and

visit some Confraternities of Charity, which had been established on the outskirts of Paris and with the working of which
he was dissatisfied? Gladly she agreed to do so. " It will
be quite sufficient," Vincent wrote to her, " if you remain
one or two days in each place on the first visit, and you can
return next summer, if Our Lord allows you, to see if you
can render Him some other services."

The task was well suited to her. She had penetration and
judgment, and she could handle people easily. She was gifted
also with Vincent's capacity for organisation. Vincent said
little of her work, but he showed his appreciation of it by
increasing it, and when a Confraternity of Charity was established in Paris, she had much to do with the management of
it. Her days were very full now, and her house was full also,
for already—though unknown either to her or to Vincent—
the foundation was being laid there of Vincent's great Order
of Sisters of Charity.

For some time Vincent had been coming across during
his missionary travels village girls, or girls described as belonging to " the lower middle class," who did not feel called to be
nuns, but who wanted to live a life of service. None of the
doors now open to women with similar longings was open
then, and the reality of the need few would have understood.
Vincent understood it, however, and so did Louise, who having
come across many of these girls also, presently opened her
house in Paris to receive into it as many of them as that house
would hold. She taught them to cook and sew and gave them
training in real nursing. They visited, like her, the sick poor
in their homes, living together under a quasi-religious rule.
Then with the establishment of that Paris Confraternity of
Charity their work began to be more widely known and was
immensely increased.

Louise had had many friends during those years when she
lived so fashionably in Paris, and these still remained her
friends. The work which she was doing interested them, and
when the Paris Confraternity of Charity was established,
numbers of them joined it. And they did so full of eagerness,
knowing that there was, indeed, much evil in the capital
waiting to be remedied. At the Hôtel Dieu, for instance, the
vast hospital of the capital, conditions were so bad as to be

hardly credible. Some twenty thousand patients were admitted to it each year, far too many for the capacities of a small, over-worked staff of nuns, a few priests and some visiting doctors. Little was known about hygiene and the overcrowding of the wards was so great that often six people slept in a bed which was meant for only two. Mattresses of straw or feather were seldom shaken and bed-clothes seldom changed. There was no isolation of infectious cases, and a woman with a newly-born baby might find herself beside a case of smallpox.

Spasmodic efforts to alter these conditions had already been made and Vincent had also been approached to do something to remedy them. He had refused, however, since such conditions, as he rightly pointed out, were no affair of his. " I have neither position nor authority," he said " to check abuses which may exist at the Hôtel Dieu as they exist everywhere else." The matter was closed so far as he was concerned and he would not speak of it again, until the Archbishop of Paris approached him also with what amounted to a command that he should help. His response then was immediate, and calling upon Louise, he and she made a further appeal to that same group of Louise's friends and other rich members of the Court to help, especially with the Hôtel Dieu. They agreed to do so, and their numbers mounted so swiftly that Vincent presently banded all together—with a simple set of rules to guide them—under the title of Ladies of Charity. The title well suited them. Their riches were colossal and their generosity—as their subsequent history proved—was almost boundless.

A new and startling experience was theirs as they crossed for the first time the threshold of the hospital. In a moment then they were plunged into the very heart of its life—its poverty, its misery, its tremendous suffering, all of which became their own.

Their work at first was mainly spiritual. Patients, who were gravely ill or in special need of help, were pointed out to them and they visited them. Then, as they realised how much could be done by the expenditure of some of their wealth on extra food, on clothing, on stipends for more priests, their purses were opened and seldom closed again.

" You cannot imagine how many persons of high rank are now visiting, instructing and exhorting the sick in the Hôtel Dieu," Vincent wrote, " behaving there in the most admirable manner and also with perseverance! Certainly those who have not seen it can hardly believe it, and all who do see it are edified, for as a matter of fact, such a life is the life of saints who serve our Lord in His members and in the best possible way."

There was certainly sanctity here, fostered unceasingly by Vincent himself, for, in the midst of his crowded life, he found time to meet these Ladies every week he was in Paris, to hear reports from them of their work and to give them little sermons " when he communicated to them, by his moving language, that love of the poor which filled his own heart."

The lives they led were truly dedicated and must have been nearly as full as Vincent's own, for the calls of family and home and of society Vincent would never allow them to leave unanswered, while he insisted also that much prayer should be interwoven with all they were doing at the hospital. Such work, he was never tired of insisting, had no value without the work of prayer as well. But eager though they were, and filled though they might be with the spirit of dedication, the demands the work made upon them were so great that they could not possibly meet them all. They applied then at last, and almost of necessity, to Louise de Marillac to give them help from that little company of girls living beneath her roof, and she acquiesced at once.

The girls themselves were younger and also much stronger than most of the Ladies of Charity. They had lived hard lives and knew, through Louise's training, something of real nursing. They had freedom and also—a big consideration from the point of view of the hospital—they could be ordered about as great Court ladies never could be ordered, in spite of their very real humility. The girls of course agreed to do anything required of them. So now their sturdy, little figures began to be well known in Paris, even though they wore as yet no distinctive dress, since they were not a community— no vows bound them. They were just a company of " country maidens," inspired by a love of God and of the poor, whom they already called their " masters " to do this work for both.

And in all they did Vincent and Louise were their directors

and close friends. Vincent loved them already. They came mostly from that good peasant stock which was his own, and he was thus at home with them as with no others. He admired them. The work they were doing was what he would have done had he been in their place. He understood their difficulties and weaknesses so well that when he talked to them, he did so as one of themselves, and always lovingly, gently and with great humour.

" Yes, indeed, you must obey the Ladies of Charity in all that concerns the services which you render to the poor," he would tell them. Then bringing his gift for mimicry into play, he would copy the reply which was so likely to be made to him by the girls. " ' But they give us so many orders! They want us to be in four places at the same time, and after we have brought the soup to the sick to go and do what they want! ' O, Sisters," and he would relapse into his former gravity, " I do not say that you should attempt to do what is impossible ; but do your best to please the Ladies, remembering that an action performed from obedience sheds a ray of light that reaches to heaven. Yet it is not enough even to obey ; you must obey in the right way, taking what is ordered you with good grace and a gay heart. For the Ladies love and esteem you highly, and their love and respect must never be abused."

Plague swept Paris in 1631, the year before Vincent went to Saint Lazare. It was one of the worst outbreaks ever known and many thousands died of it. The very word filled people with so much dread that all who could fly from the city did so. But Louise and her girls remained behind, visiting as a matter of course the worst cases and the districts which were the most infected. One of them died as a result of her labours in the Hôtel Dieu, but Louise and the rest of them survived, and Vincent did too in spite of being ready to hear the whispered confessions of the dying.

So many girls were now coming to Louise for training that it is difficult to know how her house could hold them all, and as she watched them, she became more and more convinced that they should be formed into some sort of community or company. But whenever she approached Vincent with the project, he always waved it aside.

She wanted, for instance, to make the training of them her life-work, to become their superior, living under vows. Vincent, however, refused to entertain the idea. "As for this proposal you make, Mademoiselle, I beg you once and for all not to think of it again until such time as our Lord should make it appear that He wishes it. At this moment He gives me no indication of this being His will, rather the contrary. So for His sake, Mademoiselle, let your heart honour the tranquillity of our Lord's heart, and it will be in a fit and proper spirit to serve Him."

And Louise must perforce obey, but she did so at no little cost. She had always wanted to be a nun and had even promised herself to the cloistered life before her marriage, the fact that she had not kept her promise being at the root of her frequent depression and scrupulosity. Were she to be allowed to take the threefold vow, peace would be hers, she knew.

But still Vincent held back. Never assuredly has there been " a greater apostle of delay " than was he. In 1632, when he moved into Saint Lazare, the girls were still held by no rules, save those which Louise had devised for them, and she was still living as Mademoiselle Le Gras—a widow lady without any religious status. The time was fast approaching, however, when all this would be changed, and she would become—in her own quiet, unspectacular way—something of the same great force in Paris which Vincent had become already.

CHAPTER VII

Work at Saint Lazare

WHEN Vincent moved into Saint Lazare on that January day of 1632 he found a situation which demanded no little tact. Monsieur Le Bon and his ten shadowy monks— the position of whom, as Vincent was well aware, was extremely difficult—were awaiting them. Yesterday the building had been theirs, today it was in the far more competent hands of another. Monsieur Le Bon was touchy, and Vincent, commenting on this some years afterwards, notes how carefully he had to treat him, never failing to show him the greatest respect. Thus, on his return from his missions or any other journey which took him from Paris, his first visit would be to the chapel, his next to the Prior. He supped with him every Sunday, and tried in other ways to consider his every wish. Monsieur Le Bon, however, remained a difficulty, and Vincent was frequently obliged to apologise to him as much for his own conduct as that of his sons. " I had to go and throw myself at his feet and ask pardon for all those who had in any way displeased him. He then used to grow calm, but if something else happened, the whole business had to be gone through all over again. I think he must have seen me at his feet more than fifty times. But should I not have been there? It was, indeed, quite right." And in the end Monsieur Le Bon accepted his position in a way that revealed both dignity and generosity. Later he made Vincent " heir of all his possessions."

But Monsieur Le Bon did not provide the only difficulty offered by Vincent's new position. There was the task of reorganising a building which had been allowed for so many years to fall into disrepair, and there were also the many added burdens which he of necessity must shoulder now.

Previously he had refused to take any part in those retreats given to young priests and ordinands at the Collège des Bons Enfants ; but now he could no longer refuse. " It is our will," wrote the Archbishop of Paris, " that at each of the four seasons of the year Monsieur Vincent de Paul and his Congregation should for a fortnight—but without hindrance to their missions—receive and provide for the candidates for ordination in the diocese of Paris." Such candidates, he added further, were to be " taken through the spiritual exercises."

Here was a clearly indicated work handed to Vincent and one which he was to share with his missioners, who had already become—almost equally with him—men of recognised spiritual power. Saint Lazare in its spaciousness and vast accommodation provided a fitting setting for such work and Vincent, who realised even more clearly than the Archbishop or anyone in Paris, the importance of it, now threw himself whole-heartedly into it. The Archbishop had indicated that it was not to interfere with his mission work, and although it must of necessity do so to a certain extent, still the retreats, though tending to increase in numbers and in length, were not continual. Moments did come when he could leave behind him Saint Lazare and the teeming streets of Paris for the freedom of the country and contact with the peasantry he loved.

What his missioners thought of the new work thus laid upon them we do not know, but Vincent made the importance of it very clear to them. Retreats at Saint Lazare were meant to provide a deep and searching experience for those attending them. They were not to be undertaken lightly, as assuredly they were not undertaken lightly by those responsible for them. The prayers of the whole house would be concentrated on each one, while each retreatant had a missioner of Vincent's delegated to look after him. "And if you are yourselves filled with that which is divine," Vincent told any of those missioners who might feel a shrinking from the task, " and if each one of you is struggling after perfection, then, though you may seem to have no capacity for helping these gentlemen, yet God will be able to give you help to light them on their way." Then to those who thought themselves perhaps unsuited to the work for quite other reasons, he commented in no uncertain terms that they were not to consider themselves in any way superior to those committed to their care. " For these young men," he would add, " are mostly more learned than we are. Several are bachelors and some licentiates in theology, others are doctors of Canon Law, and there are few who have not studied philosophy and a little theology. Scarcely anything that we can say to them is new. They have already either heard or read it all. They say themselves that this is not what effects them here, but the virtues which they see practised in this place."

Those last words were said by Vincent some years later, when the concentrated care given to these young men was beginning to bear fruit. Now, at what was almost the beginning of the venture, it was a more motley crowd that he and his missioners found facing them. Many of them had chosen the priesthood from worldly reasons, seeing it, if they were intelligent, as a step to high preferment. For others it had been arranged by family and friends. Some were well educated, others had scarcely any education, and few, it is safe to say, had any understanding of what a vocation to the priesthood really meant. And to them it was Vincent's task to preach—this tall, dark priest with his penetrating eyes, his air of reserve and dignity, his quick smile which could light up his whole face so surprisingly, and whose message was so astonishing in its hardness and austerity. Never, indeed, had those who heard it been presented with such an ideal of the priesthood as he set up, and it came to them from no mere visionary, but from one deeply experienced in all the activities of the state of which he spoke.

He, with his obvious gifts for drama, could have made the new life opening out before them sound the most thrilling in the world; but instead he pointed them away from any possible excitement in it, and from the intoxicating thought of any possible success, to God, and their entire surrender to Him and to His will for them. Only in such bare and naked service could they begin to understand what was meant by the dedicated life and the spirit of detachment—two things which he had learned himself at no small cost from the lips of de Bérulle and Francis de Sales. They were all to be, he told them, just slaves of God, working for Him, in Him and with Him, never allowing a thought of self to cloud their dedication.

" We must empty our hearts of all longing save for conformity with Jesus Christ and of every wish save that we may be obedient to Him. The desire to be well-thought-of—what is it other than a desire for different treatment than was accorded to the Son of God? How was He content to be regarded by the people? As a mad-man, a rebel, a fool, a sinner. Sometimes one sees one's listeners so moved by what one has said that they are all in tears. And at that it is one's instinct to be pleased. Vanity shoots up and will grow strong if one does not crush it and look solely for the glory of God, for which only we must work. For on any other terms we preach ourselves and not Jesus Christ." Then with characteristic sanity, he would condemn any dwelling on morbid, personal unworthiness. " Consider rather God's munificence in your regard than your own unworthiness in His sight, and live in His strength, rather than in thoughts of your own weakness." For the heart of his message was the age-old one of constant, unending dying to self. " Forsake thyself and thou shalt find Me," Thomas à Kempis had written years before. " You should be nought but a pure capacity for God," de Bérulle had enjoined, " clinging to Him, filled with Him."

He preached to these young men each evening of the fifteen days which the retreats lasted, and he was accessible at other times to all who were staying in the house, and many came to him for counsel. His rich humanity attracted them and his understanding, besides the depth of his experience. By the end of 1632 it was obvious that this venture at Saint Lazare had been a success, and at the end of the following year he could write thus to a fellow priest:

" You must know that during the summer the goodness of God has bestowed on our ordination exercises a great blessing, so great as to be beyond belief. For those who have been through them—or almost all—are leading lives such as a good priest should lead. There are some—notable either for their birth or for other qualities given them by God—who live as strictly by rule as we do here, and are more spiritual than many of us—more so, for instance, than I am myself. They have a time-table and are regular in mental prayer, in saying Mass, in self-examination, even as we are. They devote themselves to visiting hospitals and prisons, where they preach and catechise and hear confessions; they do this also in the colleges, and are very specially blessed in doing it."

And those described thus by Vincent, men who had been able to receive his message and carry it with them into the world, carried with them also, not only his great vision of the priesthood, but equally an awareness of the dignity which should be the outward marks of its service. All points of ritual were observed with the utmost care at Saint Lazare during the retreats. "Ceremonies may be shadows," Vincent noted to his missioners, "but they are the shadows of great truths, and it is essential that they should be carried out here with the greatest possible attention while these young men are with us. How can they be expected to observe them, if we do not perform them well ourselves? Our chanting should be done quietly and modestly; the psalms should be sung devoutly."

This same summer of 1633, when Vincent was writing so happily about the work, saw a recognition of it, which brought him added joy. There was formed then what came to be known as *Les Conférences du Mardi*, an association of young priests who met at Saint Lazare every Tuesday of the year, there to discuss problems and interests connected with their work. Vincent presided over these discussions which were of value, not only because of what he said at them, but also because of the contact each member had with others of his own generation.

The idea for them was not Vincent's. It came at the suggestion of one who had been an ordinand under his direction, and he was delighted with it. "O sir," he wrote to him, "what reasons there are for hoping that this Company will effect much good." And the hope was realised. Its members grew increasingly. Later Bossuet, the great preacher and bishop, was to be found amongst them, also Monsieur Olier, the founder of Saint Sulpice and Monsieur Tronson, his successor. The influence, indeed, which radiated over Paris from these meetings could hardly be exaggerated, and Bossuet, writing years after of Vincent's connection with them, noted him as " the founder and soul of them. We heard him, whenever he spoke, with the utmost eagerness." A variety of different subjects was arranged for discussion, while an annual retreat of all members was always held.

Something tangible was at last being done to bring about reforms for which Vincent and others so greatly longed. It was small by comparison with what was needed, but still a definite step forward had been made. Vincent still kept a hold upon the Collège des Bons Enfants and started after a little while a seminary there for boys, but the venture was not successful, and it was only some years later that the real Lazarist seminaries came into being.

But in every other way success seemed now to be crowning everything that Vincent did. The Company of his missioners was growing, so was the Company of Sisters under Louise's guidance and his direction. The Archbishop of Paris would have been the first to laud him for all that was happening at Saint Lazare. And Vincent, with his keen intelligence, recognised such success as clearly as everybody else. His reaction towards it, however, was that of fear rather than elation. He accepted it, but with shrinking, since the Christ, whom he loved and tried to imitate every moment of the day, had tasted so little of success throughout His life. Why then should he receive it at every turn? Yet such success, he forced himself to feel, must be the will of God for him, and something, therefore, to be accepted with simplicity and even joy. It remained, nevertheless, a source of ever-deepening fear to him. " He was disciplined," it has been said " by his moments of outward triumph." Any failure that ever came to him he would emphasise, while drawing attention always, and sometimes with wearisome monotony, to his own shortcomings.

His personal life now, as always, was one of extreme asceticism. He rose at 4 o'clock, and no moment of the day was empty until nightfall. Physically of course he was very strong, and coming from a tough race, had been used to toughness all his life. He asked much of himself and he asked much of others too, though he could often extend to others a tenderness which he never gave himself.

It seems a far cry from the training of priests and the preaching of country missions to the care of foundling children ; but the life of Vincent abounds in contrast, partly because his nature was so many-sided, his sympathies so wide. This particular work has earned for him spectacular and lasting fame, though actually Louise de Marillac had more to do with its administration than he had. An immense amount of money was needed to cope with the evil, and he—always a beggar of genius—was able to charm it from the rich of Paris. But with Louise lay the endless problems and difficulties inseparable from the care of tiny babies—their nurses, their food, their accommodation. Moments came when even her fine spirit and patience were taxed almost beyond endurance. Yet the evil was so terrible that in the end she was ready to accept any sacrifice to lessen it.

Its full horror she had known before it came to Vincent's notice, and he, when he learned of it, held back as usual from trying to combat it. She, however, who was so essentially maternal, could not do so, and started as soon as she was fully aware of what was really happening, to take some of these unwanted babies into her already overcrowded house.

The evil was of long-standing, and was so well known that it had been for some time a subject of legislation. Several hundreds of children were abandoned each year in the capital. They would be hidden in the dark corners of streets or laid on the steps of Notre Dame, where charitable appeals were often made for them. On all great feast-days a cot would be fastened to the pavement, several babies lying in it, while a voice called out monotonously beside it—*Faites bien à ces enfants trouvées.*

At length a law was passed decreeing that the children should be brought to a house quite near Notre Dame, known as La Couche. It was under State control and was ruled by " three respectable married women." On paper it seemed to be satisfactory, but in fact it was the opposite, its whole history being most dark and evil. Its owners, so far from being " respectable," were in close touch with the underworld of Paris. Completely without mercy for the children brought to them, they would sell them to beggars, who would mutilate them in order to incite charity, while others would be sold for the purposes of black magic, rife in the city at this time. Any baby who disturbed these women by its cries would be given laudanum; the majority not thus disposed of, would die of hunger.

The whole position regarding them was fraught with difficulty, and real reform only began to be made when Vincent's interest at last was kindled. He wrote then to a certain Madame Goussault, one of the greatest and the richest of the Ladies of Charity, and she arranged to hold a meeting in her house for discussion on the subject. " I should be very glad if you could assist at it," Vincent wrote to Louise. "Ask Madame Goussault to send her carriage for you."

The carriage was sent, the meeting was held and the first beginnings of this great work of mercy inaugurated. Some two years passed, however, before any satisfactory results became apparent, and the reform was managed so quietly that few in Paris knew of what was happening. La Couche was not even shut down. Only a gradual emptying of its pitiful inmates was made, as one after another was singled out and handed to the care of a Lady of Charity. Louise, however, eventually became responsible for them all, a burden which cost her much in the way of money and made more demands upon her time and energy, and those of her " maidens ", than any other ever asked of her or them. For the service entailed was unending. All the babies were weak and sickly. Night as well as day had to be sacrificed to them, so that it is small wonder that the girls should sometimes break down beneath the weight of their work. Vincent had to enjoin them very often to be patient.

" ' What! Am I to look after dirty, squalling brats, the children of wicked mothers who brought them into the world while offending God, and then abandoned them ? ' It is true, my daughters, that the work is very troublesome, but in the case of those who serve little children, the pain is followed by such a great reward that the trouble involved should be greatly loved. In the world you would have been mothers, but not such as you are now, for these little ones belong so entirely to God that we may call them His children, since nobody else renders them the office of father. If these were fashionable children, I mean children of distinguished families, you would have much trouble with them, and for what recompense? Very paltry salaries and you would be looked upon as servants. But what will you receive for having tended these children abandoned by all? God, throughout all eternity. O my daughters, is there any comparison? The only way to overcome difficulties when they arise is to see God in these babies."

So important did Vincent consider the service that he presently found time to make out a detailed time-table of the girls' work for their charges, from the first moment of their entry into the room where the children lay until the moment when they left them. He was interested in each one of the babies, and when they died, as they so often did, he would sometimes shed tears for them, and then console himself with the simple reflection that their deaths had added to the number of child-angels already in heaven!

The work seems to have passed comparatively unnoticed in his day; but subsequent generations, seeing the touch of drama in it, have tended to dramatise and magnify his part in it. He has been described as creeping out of Saint Lazare at night to rescue these foundlings, while pictures have been painted of him striding through drifts of snow with babies hidden beneath the folds of his voluminous cloak. Neither is true, though the tender love he gave the children, and the help he was instrumental in bringing them would be difficult to over-estimate.

CHAPTER VIII

The Sisters of Charity

IT was nearly three years after Vincent de Paul became head of Saint Lazare that he at last granted to Louise de Marillac her heart's desire and allowed her to take the threefold vow. He had already constituted her Superior of the girls whom she had been training for so long—a step which was forced upon him by reason of their numbers and widely scattered work. Their lack of " coherence " then, as Louise's contemporary biographer notes, had become a weakness. " They had no link to bind them together, no Superior in common to direct them; thus they were often found wanting in their service of the sick. For this reason Monsieur Vincent judged it necessary to unite the girls in a community under the guidance of a Superior in whom he had recognised for many years consummate prudence, exemplary piety and an ardent and indefatigable zeal. He committed to Louise de Marillac the charge of the girls, who were to live in community under her roof. She founded the Community on November 29, the vigil of Saint Andrew, 1633."

Thus came into being what was to prove the greatest perhaps of Vincent's many great achievements, though everything to do with it had happened so gradually that he had little idea himself at this time of its final magnitude. He had " no formal design " even now in regard to it. " Make no mistake, my daughters," he told some sisters years afterwards, " we never had a formal design of founding your Company. God alone formed it. I never thought of it. Your Sister Superior never thought of it for you. Accordingly, God it is of whom we can say that He was the Founder of your Company, as in truth we can find no other."

Events began to move now with what must have seemed

surprising swiftness to Louise, for on the Lady Day of the following year she was allowed to take her threefold vow, and thus became a nun, her youthful promise kept at last. Eight years, however, were to pass before any of her daughters were allowed to follow her example. Another Lady Day, that of 1642, saw the profession in Paris of four of them, their vow being then, as now, for a year, the words they uttered being the same as those which they still utter today.

" I, the undersigned, in the presence of God, renew the promise of my baptism, and make the vows of poverty, chastity and obedience to the Venerable Superior General of the Priests of the Mission in the Company of the Sisters of Charity, that I may bind myself all this year to the service—bodily and spiritual—of the poor and sick, our masters. And this by the aid of God, which I ask through His Son Jesus Christ crucified, and through the prayers of the Holy Virgin."

Vincent always laid great stress on the fact that the vow should only be yearly, and also that the Company thus formed should continue to be un-cloistered. The girls, he insisted, must be free to go about the world unfettered, in which they would offer sharp contrast to other nuns of the day, who were mostly contemplative and always enclosed. Francis de Sales had once conceived of such an order and had tried to start one, but had failed in the attempt. Vincent, who had never felt himself called to establish anything of the kind, found this little Company growing of itself before him, until in the end he was forced to stabilise it. His whole spirit, however, was woven inextricably through it, as can be seen in the beautifully chosen words with which he once described it :

" It is a Community who have no monastery but the houses of the sick, who have for cells only a lodging or the poorest room, whose chapel is the parish church and who have the streets for cloisters. They are enclosed only by obedience, they make the fear of God their grille, and they have no veil but their own modesty."

And the girls, who were prepared to accept the life thus portrayed, must never consider themselves Religious in the accepted sense, he counselled further, nor should they ever consort with members of religious communities. Strange advice, it would seem, from one who was himself always so

closely in touch with the Order of the Visitation! "Leave
the grandeur of religious women to themselves. Esteem them
highly, but do not frequent their company; their particular
spirit is not suitable for you." Then knowing that a touch
of superiority would always mark the attitude of the contemplative nun towards them, who were unenclosed, he adds
his own conviction that there were no nuns anywhere of whom
God demanded more than He did of them.

"Your vocation is one of the greatest that I know of in
the Church. And God has chosen you, poor ignorant girls,
for such a great task. Do not be astonished to such a degree
as to be proud of it, for as a rule God chooses the roughest and
most unsuitable instruments for the accomplishment of the
greatest things. When you serve those little children, when
you nurse the sick poor, you are honouring the life of our
Lord Jesus Christ, who often did the same things you do. . . .
You, my Sisters, serve those who are brought to you, and
those whom you must seek. It can truly be said of you, as
of the Apostles, that you go from one place to another, and
that just as they were sent by Our Lord, so are you also in
His Name by order of your Superior, to the end that you
should do what Our Lord Himself did upon earth. O, my
daughters, if this is the call to you, realise how greatly you
need to seek perfection. . . . You go to the poor in their
own homes and visit those who are dying without any assistance because they dare not ask for it. In this you are doing
what Our Lord did. He had no home of His own. He went
from town to town, from village to village and cured all those
whom He met. Does that not show you, my Sisters, the
greatness of your vocation? To do what God did upon
earth! Should you not be most perfect!"

The girls now started to be known as Sisters of Charity,
a name which has been theirs ever since. Then, two years
later, in 1644, full Archiepiscopal approval was given to the
Company, but not until 1656 were Letters Patent issued
granting the sanction of both Church and Crown to its
establishment and placing it for all time under the authority
of the Mission Priests. Louise had had to make a hard fight
for that last concession, Vincent having been quite ready to
surrender the Company to episcopal authority. Louise, more

clear-eyed, saw that unity between it and the Mission Priests was essential and at last Vincent saw this too.

The Company was living now quite close to him. It had moved some years before from Louise's Paris house to La Chapelle, a short distance from the capital, then in 1641 Vincent was at last able to present Louise with a house which was in all ways suitable for herself and her daughters. It was exactly opposite Saint Lazare. He had lately acquired it and now rented it to Louise. It was large, though the parish of which it was a part was one of the poorest of the capital, consisting of " vacant lots and obscure lanes, where a whole population sought refuge, driven back by misery from the centre of the city." The curé of it gave Louise the warmest welcome, and the two had soon started schools and catechisms. By this time the figures of Louise and of her daughters were familiar to all.

The girls wore now thick dark blue dresses and white collars, a white handkerchief round their heads. Their shoes were thick and their hands uncovered, and it was thus that they went about their work. They rose at the same hour as Vincent himself, and after Mass and prayer and breakfast started forth on their work of nursing, treading their way to the Hôtel Dieu and the hovels of the poor through narrow, evil-smelling streets. These last, paved with cobble-stones laid point upwards, were often made almost impassable by heavy rains or snow. Their mornings were fully occupied until twelve o'clock dinner, after which were lessons in reading, or needlework, or more nursing. There was also much time given to prayer, until at nine o'clock all went to bed.

Their lives were strenuous and yet the girls were extraordinarily happy, it being Vincent's wish that they should be so. Louise was a real mother to them and they all loved her ; she encouraged freedom and lack of constraint amongst them, and Vincent did the same. He was in close touch with them, as we have seen, and had started some years previously to give them each week short conferences or sermons, many of which are still preserved—written out in Louise's own clear handwriting—in the mother-house of the Sisters of Charity in Paris. And looking at them, and still more in reading them, a breath of the past comes to us, and we can see as in a picture rows of girls, their work-hardened hands upon their laps, listening with sparkling eyes and often with sudden gusts of laughter to the priest who was addressing them.

He was a man of over sixty in 1642, though he looked older, his hair being nearly white. Slowly and very simply he would talk to the girls, carrying on often the same imaginary conversations between himself and someone else, just as he used to do long years ago at Clichy. The girls were all a little shy of him at first, but after a short while they became so much at home with him that they would talk to him and ask him questions, conduct which delighted him. He often praised them and less often scolded them, for running through each one of his recorded conferences is a thread of admiration for the lives which they were leading, more Christ-like, as it seemed to him, than any others that he knew.

Their enforced early rising alone constituted something which he recognised as being a practice of greatest difficulty, and he often referred to it. " It frequently happens that I do not myself sleep at night," he said one afternoon, " yet I always rise at four o'clock, which is the hour fixed for the Community, for I know by experience that I should easily grow accustomed to getting up late. Hence, my dear Sisters, do a little violence to yourselves, and you will soon find it very easy, because our bodies are like asses ; accustomed to one road, they will always follow it. But to render this habit easy, make it a rule to go to bed at the right time."

His practical advice as to how they should behave towards the foundlings and the Ladies of Charity we have already seen, and he was equally practical when he touched on the spiritual aspect of their lives. " Surely," he would impress upon them, " to converse with God for half an hour is only the most delightful thing that anybody could be asked to do. Oh, how easy, and what a happiness! As a rule, people are very happy to be able to speak to a king ; those who find it hard to speak to God for half an hour have no discernment. Then to read some chapter of a devout book, O my daughters, you must never fail to do that. It is very easy and most necessary, for as in the morning you speak to God when at prayer, so God speaks to you when you read. It is also easy to make a particular examen before supper, and before going to bed to make a general examination of conscience, then to retire to rest at nine o'clock, and to go to sleep with a good thought in your mind."

The Sisters' new house possessed an oratory, but Mass was seldom said in it, the Sisters always going across the road to the church of Saint Lazare. The lights which suddenly shone forth from each building at four o'clock each morning must have been something of a surprise to any chance passer-by.

The ages of the girls presenting themselves for admission to the Company varied between eighteen and twenty. Louise preferred country girls to those brought up in towns, the latter being more sophisticated and more difficult to train. And she looked askance at any who were very grave, or who took themselves very seriously, or who were inclined towards melancholy. " The melancholy type of mind is very odd," wrote Vincent once in comment on the last. And, indeed, a great joy was the hall-mark of the whole community. *Toujours gai et content!* was a little phrase often applied to Louise and it fitted her daughters too. " My Sister," Vincent asked one of them as she lay dying, " is there anything in your past life that makes you fear death ? " To which she gave the surprising answer—" No, Father, except that I have taken too great pleasure in my work. When I went about the villages, I felt such joy in serving the people of them, that it seemed to me as if I had wings and flew about." The answer delighted Vincent. " It behoves Sisters," he said, " to manifest to others the joy which should appear on their faces as well as hidden in their hearts. When one has joy in one's heart, it cannot be concealed, it can be seen clearly on the face. When you serve the sick, you should serve them in such a way that joy is visible on your countenance."

And yet all occasions of ordinary earthly joy were forbidden them. They must not only refuse gifts from any whom they tended but also even gratitude. They must never stop to speak to anyone whom they might meet upon their way as they went out visiting. No feeling of elation or of satisfaction in their work might ever be encouraged. Their rule was so strict that they might never go outside their mother-house without permission, nor return without reporting their return.

And complete " custody of the eyes " must always be theirs, the last a specially difficult discipline for country girls to whom the sights of Paris were a continual excitement. One of them confessed once how she could only prevent herself from gazing at the peep-shows and troupes of performers, which she sometimes met, by pressing her crucifix against her heart and murmuring—" O Jesus, Thou art worth it all."

All reliance upon great friendships was discouraged, and more particularly on great friendships with priests. " Mistrust confessors more than anybody else," Vincent said to them one day. " There is nothing so dangerous as attachment to confessors, and as soon as you see that you are taking pleasure in going to one and find it hard to go to another, you may say, ' I am caught! ' and you must go to someone else. ' But such a one does not satisfy me,' you will say. ' Another does not say a word to me. I am greatly helped by this one's guidance.' Nonsense, Sisters, nonsense! It is not the confessor who is the cause of your advancement, it is God." Always it was God! Seek God! Lean on God! Leave all to God! " For whom are you seeking? " a Sister was asked once as she was visiting amongst the poorest hovels of Paris. " I am seeking Jesus Christ," was her surprising answer.

Vincent commented often on the girls' Rule during those conferences, which were held always in the spotless parlour of their house across the road. The keeping of it was of such infinite importance and yet their work of nursing the sick must always take precedence of it, for " to nurse the sick is to pray."

One day at the conclusion of his discourse a Sister stood up and said that she was afraid she had broken the Rule on several occasions lately. One or two others followed her example, and as they sat down, Vincent spoke again. " I pray God with all my heart to forgive you your failings, my daughters." he said. "And I ask you for your forgiveness for myself. For I, wretched man that I am, do not keep my own rules. I am very guilty in your regard in all that concerns your work. Pray to God, I implore you, to have mercy on me. And for my part, I will pray Our Lord Jesus Christ to impart to you Himself His holy benediction, and I shall not pronounce the words of blessing today, for the faults which

I have committed in your regard render me unworthy to do
so. I, therefore, pray Our Lord to give it." And kneeling
down, we are told, he kissed the ground. Upon which Louise
de Marillac begged him, in the name of all the Sisters, not to
refuse his blessing, and she insisted so strongly that he agreed.
" Pray then to God," he said, " not to look upon my unworthiness or on the sins of which I am guilty, but that,
having mercy on me, He may pour forth His blessings upon
you, whilst I pronounce the words."

The Rule was read every Friday, and adherence to it made
a claim on every hour of the day. But without it, and its
almost incredible hardness, this strange little Order could
not possibly have existed. The streets of Paris in the seven-
teenth century were no place for women to tread alone ; but
Louise and her daughters trod them unmolested, entering as
a matter of course houses and hovels which the *gendarmerie*
of the day would have found excuses to avoid. Later they
were to travel over a war-swept country, facing alone a lawless
soldiery. And when one searches for the secret of their
power, one can find it only in their strict training, and the
reiterated command that self must find no place in their
scheme of life ; God was to reign alone.

Some, it is true defected, and Louise found such defections
very hard to bear, though Vincent accepted them quite calmly.
" You take the departure of your daughters rather too much
to heart," he wrote to her. " In the name of God, Mademoiselle, try to acquire grace to accept the occurrences. Our
Lord shows His mercy to the Company in purging it after
this manner, and this will be one of the first things He will
reveal to you in heaven. You must be quite certain that none
of those whom Our Lord has really summoned into the
Company will fail in her vocation. Why should you trouble
about the others ? Let them go ; we shall not lack for
daughters."

There were very few of Vincent's activities in which Louise
and her daughters played no part, and presently he made
demand of her and of them for help in that work amongst
galley-slaves, which he had begun some twenty years before.
He had never relinquished it, and now as result of continued
visits to the Paris prisons where the men still lay, he had

managed to have the many who were ill in them isolated from those who were well. Would Louise go and look after the former, he asked, and would she allow her daughters to do likewise? And without any hesitation Louise answered that she would.

Here the genius of her training is revealed in startling fashion. For the girls accepted this new work unquestioningly, even though they were visiting men, who torn for long from wives and families, were uncontrolled, undisciplined. Many people would have considered that no woman should have encountered the sights and sounds which greeted them on all sides in those dark dungeons. Yet there is no record of any of Louise's girls desiring to relinquish the work, nor yet of any of them experiencing the smallest harm. They entered the prisons only in companies of two and they always had some specific reason for going—to nurse, or to bring food, or a message from the outside world.

The lives they were leading were certainly eventful and threaded through quite often with great drama. Then the year 1635—a few months after Louise had been allowed to take her threefold vow—such drama was deepened, as the country was caught into the vortex of the Thirty Years War, one of the most savage wars of history. Its anguish and its horrors made little difference to the life of the Court in Paris, but to Louise and to her daughters, and to an even greater degree to Vincent and his sons, it came as a time of such testing and such suffering as none of them had ever experienced before. Its events also brought Vincent into unexpected limelight, and he who had known the Court only through his connection with the Ladies of Charity, was to find himself now in closest touch with King and Queen, and later with numberless courtiers amongst whom he could never feel himself as anything but an unwilling stranger.

CHAPTER IX

Vincent Goes to Court

THE King who was reigning in Paris when Vincent had first arrived there thirty-five years before, the much loved Henri IV, was murdered two years later, to be succeeded by his son, a boy of only nine years old. He was Louis XIII, and the country had for regent his Italian mother, Marie de Medici, an extravagant, foolish woman, who cared so little for her son that she was often cruel to him. He in his turn gave her no affection, and looked forward only to the moment when he could throw aside her yoke. That moment was long in coming.

She had, as regent, considerable power, which she used disastrously, and France which had been reviving under her husband's wise rule, soon sank into a parlous condition under hers. Money which should have been used by the State for the betterment of the people was spent by her on clothes and jewellery, and presents which she lavished on two worthless favourites, both of them adventurers. She was mainly influenced by them, and it was small wonder that lawlessness should break out on every side. The wars of religion were soon renewed, whilst there were constant rebellions amongst the rich and powerful nobles and princelings of the country. Thus, France internally was in chaos, while outside was a ring of enemies, intent upon the acquisition of different parts of a country, whose growing weakness was obvious to them all.

The great foreign power of the moment was the House of Hapsburg, which ruled Germany, Spain, Portugal, the Netherlands and parts of Italy. The Spanish branch of it was France's greatest enemy, for Alsace was owned by it, and it touched French borders at so many other points besides, that fear and hatred of it were deeply rooted in the hearts of every Frenchman. Both were rooted in the hearts of others also, the Spaniards being cruel rulers and still more cruel foes.

So great a concentration of power was disquieting to all Europe, and in 1618 a war to break it was started in Bohemia. France held aloof from the war at first, but as it gained momentum, she took a part in it, and then it was that Vincent was forced to step from the comparatively quiet world of Saint Lazare to the tangled world of politics.

Marie de Medici had ceased to reign the year before this war began. In 1617, the same year which saw Vincent's escape to Châtillon, her son—then a boy of sixteen—wrested by a sort of minor *coup d'état* all power from her hands. She was banished and he reigned in her stead, but his rule was no better than hers, for not only was he young and inexperienced, but he was dominated also by even more worthless favourites than those of his mother. He was already married to a girl of his own age, daughter of the King of Spain, but known as Anne of Austria. And beautiful though she was and kindly too, she was unpopular with a people, who saw her as so closely connected with their greatest enemy. Her husband's love she never won, and her marriage remained childless until twenty-three years after it was celebrated.

Extravagance and corruption reigned at the Court, while poverty grew in the country. Never had a wise ruler been more needed, and then at last one appeared—a man who was to be accounted later one of the greatest of all French statesmen, Armand-Jean du Plessis, Cardinal duc de Richelieu.

His figure had been for some years well known at Court, Marie de Medici having held him deeply in her confidence. For this reason, if for no other, the young King distrusted him, and some time passed before Richelieu could win his confidence. But when at length he did win it, his victory was complete, and a weak King and still weaker country came under his sole domination.

Love of power was the strongest trait of his complex character, but he wanted it, not for personal aggrandisement, but for France, and fully aware of the depths to which the nation had sunk, he framed at once a policy by which the nation should be raised. It was a simple one. France must first be unified, and to this end the power of the Huguenots must be broken. The warring nobles and princelings must then be reduced to obedience, after which it would be possible to turn to the rapidly strengthening Spanish menace.

The Huguenots were brave and stubborn foes, and it was not until 1628, when La Rochelle, their last stronghold was captured, that they ceased to be a danger to the country, and Richelieu found himself free to deal with the turbulent nobles. These were soon weakened, as one plot after another was discovered and the plotters punished. The latter were never wholly subdued, however, though a moment did come at last when Richelieu felt that they had been rendered sufficiently powerless for him to be able to play a part in foreign affairs. And then France went to war. It was inevitable that she should if she were to be saved from becoming a mere appendage of Spain. But the cost in misery and men and money was so great that there were many who questioned, as the war progressed, the wisdom of Richelieu's policy. He, however, ruling as a dictator now, would take advice from none.

He often followed the French troops in person, for he was at heart a soldier, but he was most often to be found in Paris where he reigned in his palace, the Palais Cardinal, which stood quite near the Louvre, in greater state even than the King. There fantastic splendour surrounded him, and he entertained in lavish fashion. His sumptuous rooms were made lovely by pictures and tapestries, furniture and china of the rarest. His great banqueting-hall was daily filled with princely guests, who having eaten and drunk food and wine of the most costly, were free then to wander about gardens which covered several acres and whose beauty was the wonder of Paris. Glittering was the only word by which to describe these crowds of courtiers, and Richelieu, dressed in his scarlet cardinal's robes, rings glistening on his fingers, made a fitting host to them. He was of fine appearance, though his health was always bad, and he suffered often bouts of acute pain of which he never spoke. In manner he was very quiet, and there were few who were not frightened of him.

France entered the war in 1635, as we have seen, and

fighting was acute not long after on her north-eastern borders. Events at first went badly for her, her troops being inexperienced in fighting on a large scale, and a moment soon came when the country was invaded. Spanish troops from the Spanish Netherlands came pouring across her frontiers soon threatening the way to Paris. The country round the Somme became then a devastated area as whole towns and villages were burned. The utmost savagery prevailed. There was no food. Crops and cattle had been wilfully destroyed and famine, so fierce that human flesh was often eaten, came as the inevitable result. Plague then followed. And through all these horrors Paris remained gay and unconcerned, with operas, balls, feasting still the order of the day.

There was no feasting, however, at Saint Lazare. Many of Vincent's missioners were living in those devastated areas and had written him descriptions of what they were seeing every day, and he was appalled. " God is afflicting his people," he said. " This is a time to do penance." And black bread instead of white was eaten henceforth at every meal at Saint Lazare. But more must be done than that and Vincent, who hated to take action unless he was forced by others to do so, took action now and started forth on a mission which cost him much to undertake. It was no less than a visit to the Palais Cardinal, there to plead with its owner for these suffering people. He did so on his knees. " My Lord, have pity on us. Let us have peace. Give peace to France." Richelieu listened. Vincent was well known to him, and he could not fail to be moved by so much anguish of sincerity; but he would do nothing. " I desire peace as much as you do, Monsieur Vincent," he replied, " but peace does not depend on me alone." Vincent could get nothing from him, and sorrowfully he went away.

But he was a fighter and the matter, he knew, must not be allowed to rest. If the root of the evil could not be attacked, at least those famine-stricken people should not be left unaided. Money must be raised to bring them food and help, and money was raised. Ladies of Charity and others of great wealth in the capital were appealed to. Then appeal was made to the King and Queen, who both responded so generously that soon large sums had been collected. And these were spent without delay on food and drink and clothes, which were packed on mules and sent to Vincent's missioners. Others besides were engaged in this work of mercy, but the missioners were chief amongst them, their knowledge of the country being so great. And as result, we learn, that " thousands of Lorrainers " were saved from death. " The sick found scattered in the woods or in streets and squares, were gathered together and nursed. The hungry were fed and the naked clothed." Detailed reports of all that was being done were frequently sent to Saint Lazare for transmission to the King and Queen and the Ladies of Charity.

But little mention was made in them of all that Vincent's missioners were daily facing. The strain upon them was so great as to be hardly bearable at times, and Vincent would have given much to have been able to go to them himself. He could not leave Saint Lazare, however, so he sent instead his Assistant Superior to give each one of them his love and sympathy and encouragement. The latter wrote movingly of conditions which he found at one of the first places which he visited, then described the experiences of the missioner there in the latter's own words.

" There are more than three hundred in great necessity," he said, " and more than three hundred in the direst need. More than a hundred look like skeletons covered with skins, and they present such a horrible appearance that if Our Lord did not give me strength, I would not dare to look at them. Their skin is like black marble and is so shrunken that their teeth are dry and uncovered, and their eyes and whole countenance have a scowling appearance. It is the most dreadful sight that can ever have been seen. They hunt about in the fields for roots which they cook and eat. Several girls are dying of hunger. Some of them are young and I fear lest despair may bring them to greater misery than that of this world." And it was not only the peasantry who were thus suffering, but the one-time rich as well.

Many of these missioners, working so quietly and heroically, died as result of their labours, which is not surprising seeing what those labours were. Under-nourished themselves, they never had time for rest, their priestly office occupying every hour of their days and much of their nights as well.

Mass and Offices must always be said, numbers of confessions heard, and the many who were dying prepared for the last Sacraments. They had no houses of their own and in many cases no churches, these having been destroyed by the troops. Then, as the war dragged on month after month, year after year extremes of heat and cold had to be faced, together with extremes of ever-mounting misery. Yet few faltered on the way. Vincent had trained them well.

And, meanwhile, money still poured into Saint Lazare. The King and Queen had set an example of generosity, and they continued to take an interest in Vincent's work. They had known of him already, the Ladies of Charity having spoken of him frequently, particularly to the Queen, who now having come into personal contact with him, was at once attracted to him. Naturally generous, she would like to have lavished money on him, but she was so extravagant that her purse was often empty, so she would send him presents of jewellery instead. Once a diamond worth 1,000 livres was brought to Saint Lazare, then a pair of ear-rings worth 1,800 livres. The gift of the latter she asked might be kept secret, but Vincent refused. " It is good that all Paris should know about it," he said, " and I shall tell about it everywhere."

And still the war dragged on. By 1642 France had been fighting for seven years, yet hostilities showed no sign of ending. The power of Spain might be weakening, but she was undefeated still. And now the Cardinal's health was failing rapidly, and it became known, as 1642 wore on, that he could not live for long. Throughout the autumn he travelled much over France, imprisoned in a litter from which he could not move without anguish. His right arm was paralysed and his whole body racked with pain. November found him at Lyons from which he set forth at length for Paris, travelling thither by slow degrees. It was to be his last journey, and back once more in the Palais Cardinal he died there on December 4.

His years of power had brought success to France, though at the price of untold suffering, and although he had won for himself a place amongst the great statesmen of history, he had won from the country fear rather than affection. " If there be a God," the Pope said when news of his death was brought to him, " the Cardinal de Richelieu will have much to answer for. If there be none, then he lived a successful life." He was buried in the chapel of the Sorbonne, which he had built, and on the cold morning his body was interred there many in Paris looked forward to the future with misgiving. For who was capable of taking up the reins of government which he had held so tightly? The King, even if he could rule alone, was known to be so ill that many had wondered if his death might not precede the Cardinal's, and his heir was only four years old.

The winter that year was so cold that there was great misery in the city, and presently the King left it for the palace of Saint Germain, where the air was purer, and there the Queen watched by him. She was forty-two, but had lost little of her beauty and nothing of the gaiety and generosity and *joie-de-vivre* which had always made up so much of her charm.

The King had fought consumption for many years. Now its onslaughts were getting the better of him, and by April he was known to be, indeed, a dying man. The Queen, fonder of him now than she had ever been, would have done anything to help him. He behaved with a courage characteristic of him, while turning continually to religion, which had always meant something to him. It always meant much to the Queen too, who now bethought herself of the mission-priest at Saint Lazare, and of the help which he in his great holiness might bring her husband. She suggested then that he should come and visit him, and Vincent came. He stayed, however, for only a short while, the King having rallied surprisingly. Then he was summoned back some three weeks after, the King being really dying then.

Bishops and priests surrounded him, yet place was given to Vincent. " What is the best preparation for death? " the King asked of him. " Sire," came the answer, " there is nothing better than the example of Our Saviour. His complete and perfect submission was testified in the words, ' Not My will, but Thine be done.' " To which the King replied— " I wish with all my heart to follow Him." Later he was heard to utter the practical reflection that if he should get well, he would order every bishop in his kingdom to stay for some time at Saint Lazare. He lingered for several days, then died on Ascension Day, May 14, 1643. It was the same date as that on which his father had been murdered thirty-three years before.

Vincent remained on in the palace at the Queen's request. Emotional always, she was filled then with genuine grief, and turned instinctively to him whom she asked now to become her guide. " Do not forsake me," she is reported to have said to him. " I place myself in your hands. Lead me in the way of perfection, for I intend to love and serve God truly." Vincent had no choice but to obey, and certainly few in the kingdom stood in greater need of direction than did she.

History was repeating itself most strangely now, for here was another Queen-Mother as regent for a king, who this time was only four years old. But whereas before there had been nobody to take up the reins of government, now somebody, whom Richelieu himself had trained in statecraft, was waiting on the alert to do so. He was another Cardinal, but an Italian, Guilio Mazarin, who would be adjudged later as " the greatest adventurer of all history."

He and Vincent were already known to one another. Nobody who ever came to Court could have failed to be aware of his flamboyant figure. The son of a Sicilian business man, he had been born in Italy, and was now about forty years of age, a man of singular charm and also of extreme good looks. He had risen to his present exalted position by reason of his keen wits and outstanding personality. " I have just been speaking to the greatest man the State has ever had," Richelieu said of him on the occasion of their first meeting. Richelieu, indeed, an astute judge of character, had recognised immediately beneath the wit and brilliancy, the love of riches and display of the handsome young Italian an intelligence of the most remarkable. Here was one who could rule when he was gone.

It was important that he and the Queen should be on friendly terms, a fact which Mazarin realised more clearly than anybody else, and to charm the Queen was not difficult. Gently and with flattery he insinuated himself into her confidence, and won his first victory when on the death of the King, she ratified his appointment as Chief Member of the Council and Minister to her son.

The friendship of the two henceforth grew deeper every day. He was given apartments of his own in the Louvre, and there he lived, while each evening he would hold a conference with the Queen, though so clever were his tactics that he arranged such conferences should always take place in public. The two would sit and talk together quite openly in front of all the passing, chattering courtiers, though it is true that none of them would ever think to intrude on Queen or Cardinal, who were thus at liberty to discuss, if they wished, other affairs than those of State. *Le Petit Conseil* was the name given to these whispered nightly conversations, which the Queen at least most obviously enjoyed. Always susceptible to men, she had now met one strong and clever enough to dominate her, and she soon began to rejoice in such domination.

But those who looked on saw little reason for rejoicing. Mazarin, who could rule the Queen so easily, could not rule the people. They saw in him only an upstart foreigner. His flashing charm, his fine clothes and above all his extravagance, even greater than that of the Queen, produced in them hostility so fierce that they were blind to the fine intelligence and statesmanlike qualities hidden beneath these other attributes.

No greater contrast could have been imagined than that offered by him to Vincent de Paul, yet now the two were to come into close contact with one another. For Vincent was appointed, at the express wish of the Queen—immediately after the death of the King—a member of the Council of Ecclesiastical Affairs, known as the Council of Conscience. It was an important post, the Council being responsible for all ecclesiastical appointments throughout the kingdom ; but it was one of extreme distaste to Vincent. For not only did it take him away from Saint Lazare and his many interests there, but it flung him also into a Court ruled by a man, who was definitely hostile to him. Mazarin, indeed, made no attempt to hide his enmity for the priest whose standards were so different from his own, and over whom he could exercise no influence. Unscrupulous always where money was concerned, he thought nothing of selling bishoprics, abbeys, benefices to the highest bidder, and as head of the

Council of Conscience, which numbered only five, he could often do so, though never without a solemn protest from Vincent. And if such protests did not always bear fruit, they were talked about nevertheless by others and people began to ponder.

Vincent announced, when first he started on this new work, that there were certain abuses in force which he would never countenance—abuses which seem to us of today to be so flagrant that his plea for their discontinuance only strikes us as most modest. Children, he said, should not be given bishoprics, nor infants in their cradles placed at the head of abbeys. A bishopric should be conferred only on one who had been a priest at least a year. A cathedral canon must be at least sixteen years of age, and a canon of a college fourteen years. There were other abuses that he named, while on the constructive side were reforms which revealed, to any who might not have known of them before, his great longing for the raising of the priesthood to the level which those now living at Saint Lazare gave proof it could attain.

The Council would meet at the Louvre, or Fontainebleau, or wherever the Court happened to be in residence. Quite often it met at the Palais Cardinal, called now the Palais Royal, for Richelieu had left it to the little King.

The way to it was soon one of the most familiar to Vincent, and it is not difficult to imagine how much he hated taking it. He, who was seldom self-conscious, became so the moment he found himself in this world which fitted him so ill. He would emphasise unnecessarily the fact of his peasant birth and his own ignorance. On the first occasion when he arrived for a conference, the Prince de Condé, one of his fellow-members on the Council and cousin to the King, pointed him to a seat quite near his own.

Vincent refused to take it. " It is already too great an honour for Your Highness to tolerate my presence," he said, " I, who am the son of a swineherd. . . ." Yet he showed no diffidence when later in the proceedings controversial points of theology and Canon Law were raised. " You tell everybody, Monsieur Vincent," Condé remarked at the end of the meeting, " and you preach everywhere that you are an ignorant man, and yet you settle the most difficult questions with two words. Her Majesty could certainly have chosen no more enlightened councillor to deal with ecclesiastical affairs."

Condé might show courtesy to him, but not so Mazarin and others. One day Mazarin pointed with astonishing ill-breeding to his poor cassock and worn-out girdle. "Look how Monsieur Vincent comes to Court!" he laughed. "See what a beautiful girdle he wears!" and he held it up for all to share his laughter.

The many demands which came from courtiers and others of the greatest in the land for bishoprics or abbeys or rich benefices Vincent would refuse, unless he thought those who made the demands were worthy of them, and such refusals often earned him the harshest treatment. Insulting remarks would be heaped upon him by people whom he regarded as too grand for companionship with him. "It is easily seen," one great lady remarked to him, "that you do not know how to treat people of quality. I have already done you too much honour by even addressing you. I know the Prince de Condé well and will obtain from him what I cannot obtain from you." On another occasion a certain duchess, who was also maid of honour to the Queen, ended her torrent of abuse of him by throwing a footstool at his head, and he left her with blood streaming down his face. The offence he had committed was the refusal of a bishopric to her son, whose moral life was the most scandalous in the neighbourhood where he lived, and who was so confirmed a drunkard that he was often picked up unconscious in the streets.

Sometimes bribes would be enclosed in the letters of request which came to him, and once the enormous sum of 100,000 livres was offered to him. "God guard me from taking this money," he said, as he looked at it, "I would rather die." Later he was told of a rumour which had been started over Paris to the effect that he had accepted a library and 600 livres in return for the gift of a bishopric. He minded this rumour so much that he took up his pen to protest against it, then refrained. But if the taking of bribes offered him no temptation, there was one of greater subtlety which needed some strength to resist—the giving of preferment to men whom he had specially trained. Conscious though he might be, however, of their worth, they were never pushed forward in any way.

But his influence on the Council tended to grow less as years passed by, for Mazarin disregarded more and more his decisions, or else summoned the Council so seldom that its power was largely gone. Yet Vincent left his mark upon it and upon the Court as well where it was held. For none who ever encountered his shabby figure there—so incongruous in such a setting—was likely to forget it. Later his memory was to be impressed upon it with even deeper strength.

CHAPTER X

Jansenism

VINCENT'S position on the Council of Conscience brought him into touch with other things besides the granting of ecclesiastical appointments, and he had hardly taken his place upon it before he was plunged into the heart of a controversy which set all Paris talking, and which was to prove a source of great danger to the Church. It was that of Jansenism, whose history in France may be difficult and tangled, but is one of importance and marked often by drama as well as interest.

Vincent had known much about it for some time, having been at first attracted to it, since many of the aims of its leaders were similar to his own—a reform of the priesthood and a deepening of real religion throughout the country. It was only as he learned more about it and touched more closely those who were its exponents that he realised its dangers and became one of its strongest enemies.

Its name was taken from Cornelius Jansen, one-time Bishop of Ypres, upon whose ideas and practices it was founded. He, a scholar of considerable note, had been early drawn to the teaching of St. Augustine, in which study he was joined by a Frenchman, the Abbé de St. Cyran. The latter, a great scholar also, and a few years younger than Vincent, came from Gascony, though there was little of Gasçon gaiety or sparkle to mark his sombre personality. His creed was sombre too, all its emphasis being placed on sin, and the necessity of its punishment and expiation.

The two would read together daily for many hours the vast number of St. Augustine's books, such narrow intensity of study inspiring them both with the conviction that the Church of the present day should be brought back to the same conditions as those prevailing in the early centuries of Christianity. These conditions, in their hardness and severity, were in direct contrast to those which marked the Paris of the moment. The laxity reigning then in the city amongst religious leaders and others filled the two with horror. " The whole world lieth in wickedness! " St. Cyran often quoted. And this vision of corruption and of uncorrected sin clouded considerably his understanding of other things. The people must be punished, he cried. Laxity amongst the clergy must cease. No leniency must ever be shown. The old-time practice of public penance must be revived, together with the practice of withholding absolution even after confession has been made.

Views so startling and presented by a man of so much force and conviction could not fail to make a stir in Paris, and this assuredly they did. St. Cyran's sincerity was patent, and hard though both he and his doctrine were, he possessed a certain charm, which even reached to Richelieu.

St. Cyran and Vincent had first come into contact with one another as far back as 1621, when Vincent was still living with the de Gondis. The two met at the house of de Bérulle and were immediately attracted to one another. Later Vincent confessed himself as having been " ravished, elevated and inflamed " by the discourses of St. Cyran. Here, indeed, was one who shared to the full so many of his own longings for reform.

St. Cyran's fame continued to grow, then was increased, as he was appointed director of the convent of Port Royal of the Fields, the story of which provides one of the strangest and also the most tragic of religious history. And that story is linked so closely with the whole history of Jansenism in France that pause must be made to sketch it in briefest outline.

The convent stood then, as its desolate ruins still stand, some twenty miles from Paris in what was at the time a lonely, snake-ridden valley. There a handful of lifeless nuns eked out a dreary existence until in 1602 a little girl of eleven was appointed as their abbess. Her name was Jacqueline Arnauld, but she took in religion the name of Angélique. Her family was a great one, being known all over Paris and beyond it because of the brilliancy and the learning of its members. But Angélique was only a frightened child when she arrived first at the great building which she had been appointed to rule. " I was wide awake and wild, more than can be conceived," she wrote years after. " I cared only to play and converse and amuse myself. All the observances of religion were distasteful to me, since my heart was not open to piety." Then, when she was seventeen, what has been described as " an awakening " came to her, and realising something of what is meant by the Religious Life, she decided that she and her nuns must start to live it. So in the face of immense opposition from her family and others, she closed and barred the gates of her convent and started to follow a rule of extreme asceticism.

Conduct so strange coming from a member of a family which was so widely known was bound to startle Paris and it did, though to create a sensation was the last thing that Mère Angélique, either then or later, wished to do. Quiet, grave and very austere, her whole life was centred on her convent to which so many girls and women began now to aspire that soon the community was obliged to move to Paris. And there she encountered St. Cyran, who became her director and director to her nuns.

The two were alike in many ways and notably in their spirituality wherein joy found no place. All emphasis was laid by them on sin. And how, they both questioned, could priests, and notably the Jesuits, allow their flocks to use the Sacraments so lightly? Flagrant sinners—the King's own brother amongst them—were given absolution and then admitted to Communion as a matter of course. Surely such conduct was sacrilegious and should not be countenanced?

But public affairs were no business of Mère Angélique's. Hers was the hidden life of a dedicated nun wherein publicity should play no part. It was ironic then that publicity should so often be hers. Her convent, which had flamed into interest years before when she started to reform it, now flamed into further interest, as a charge of heresy was brought against it by reason of a book written by one of its nuns.

The book, a devotional little treatise on prayer, was a curious one, indeed, to have provoked a controversy in which

numbers of the religious world of Paris immediately became
most deeply interested. Feeling at last became so high that
the book was submitted to the Sorbonne, who disapproved
of it. It was then despatched to Rome for the judgment of
the Pope, while Paris waited, finding in this religious fight
something quite new on which to feed its jaded appetite.
These Arnaulds always did become involved in interesting,
unusual things, and when the Abbé de St. Cyran presently
entered the lists in defence of Port Royal, interest deepened.
Would the Pope approve of his judgment or that of the
Sorbonne? And when the Pope refused to condemn the
book, St. Cyran's influence was immensely increased.

It was growing, indeed, in startling fashion. His thunder-
ing creed was everywhere attracting notice, its very hardness
giving it a sort of fascination. Its vigour also offered great
contrast to the prevailing lightness and superficiality of the
day. He made religion all at once a living thing, no longer
a mere convention. Hundreds were soon ready to hang upon
his words. Then, as those words increased in force and
fervour, there were some who started to be distrustful of
them. Amongst their numbers was Vincent de Paul.

His friendship with St. Cyran had begun to cool already,
and by the time he had settled into Saint Lazare, meetings
between the two were rare. For St. Cyran's agitation for
reform had become by then so unbalanced that Vincent could
not approve of it. St. Cyran was abusing not only the abuses
reigning in the Church but the Church itself, and already his
name was being coupled with those of Luther and of Calvin.
He believed in predestination like the latter, and he looked
also for sudden clear signs of conversion in his followers. And
these followers were now so many that Richelieu—his previous
affection for St. Cyran gone, and even more deeply disturbed
than Vincent by all that he was saying—ordered his imprisonment. " Do you know of what man you are speaking? " he
asked of one who came to intercede for him. " He is more
dangerous than six armies. Had only Luther and Calvin been
taken in such good time, we should have been spared much
trouble."

St. Cyran's imprisonment—which lasted for five years—
served rather to strengthen than to weaken his influence, which

was, indeed, far deeper than even Richelieu had guessed. The fact of it was presently proved by the sensation created by a book, published during the year of Vincent's appointment to the Council of Conscience and after St. Cyran himself was dead. It was written by Mère Angélique's youngest brother, Antoine Arnauld, a priest, a notable scholar, attached to the Sorbonne, and the most brilliant member of her brilliant family. Anything that appeared from his pen demanded notice, but neither he nor anyone else was prepared for the sensation which this book—only to be found now unread on dusty shelves—was destined to make.

Its unprovocative and not very interesting title was *Livre de la Fréquente Communion*, and it was a treatise chiefly on Communion and how often Communion should be received, the whole being based on a book by Jansen, *Augustinus*, which had appeared some years before. Emphasis upon sin marked all its pages, together with insistence that Communion should be withheld from sinners and allowed only to the very few. Four editions of the book appeared within six months of its publication, and the Court was soon discussing it. Clearly and logically arguments were built up which carried conviction to many of those who read them, and amongst others to a brilliant youth of twenty-three, Blaise Pascal by name. He was so thrilled that he laid aside all his own work for several months to concentrate only on Arnauld's arguments.

But there were others who were revolted by them, and notably the Queen, who had been brought up with a devotion to the Blessed Sacrament which never wavered at any time. The Jesuits, whose lax methods of direction Arnauld had attacked, were outraged by it, while the more deeply Vincent studied it, the more deeply he felt its danger. Here might be a sorrow similar to his own for lax and sinful clergy serving a lax and sinful world, but Arnauld's remedy for both he felt was wrong. For the Sacraments, Vincent considered, should be used by all and not set aside only for the elect few, since they possessed the greatest strength there was with which to combat evil. He was disturbed then, and frightened too, when he learned that the numbers of Communions made in Paris, even on Easter Day, were rapidly diminishing. And still Arnauld's book continued to be read. " Ladies of fashion studied it with pleasure, and were both proud and happy to be thought capable of discussing theology in their *salons*."

Presently then the influence of the book reached even to members of his own Congregation, and it was thus he wrote to one of them during the autumn of 1648—

" It may be true, Sir, as you assert that some persons in France and Italy have benefited by this book, but for a hundred here in Paris who may perhaps have so benefited by its teaching, rendering them more reverential in their frequentation of the Sacrament of Holy Communion, there are at least ten thousand who have been injured by it, causing them to abstain altogether from approaching the Altar."

Referring then to Arnauld's advocacy of public penance, he notes :

" We know that throughout Europe the Sacraments are administered in the manner condemned by Monsieur Arnauld, and that the Pope and all the bishops approve of the custom of imparting absolution after confession, and of exacting public penance only for public sin. Is it not intolerable blindness to prefer to the universal practice of the whole Christian world— and in a matter of so much consequence—the ideas of a young man who was, when he wrote this book, without any experience in the guidance of souls ? "

Then turning to Arnauld's assumption that what he is advocating is only something to deepen love and adoration for the Blessed Sacrament, he fiercely condemns such contention.

" Monsieur Arnauld infers," he writes, " that Jesus Christ can only be outraged and put to shame by our frequent Communions, and this by reason of our unworthiness." But who, Vincent cogently inquires, is worthy ? "As for myself, I frankly confess that if I had a high opinion of Monsieur Arnauld's book, I would not only renounce for ever in a spirit of humility Holy Mass and Communion, but I should also be in terror of the Sacrament, regarding it, according to the book, as a snare of Satan, and as poison to those who receive it under the usual conditions that the Church approves. Can, indeed, any man be found on this earth with such a high opinion of his own virtue as to think he is in a fit state to receive Holy Communion worthily ? Such a position is held by Monsieur

Arnauld alone, who, having made the necessary conditions so difficult that St. Paul might have feared to approach, does not hesitate to tell us that he himself says Mass every day."

It is seldom that we find Vincent writing with so much urgency, but Arnauld's book had filled him with a sort of horror as well as with fear, and now he spared no effort, as member of the Council of Conscience, to prevent the spread of its doctrines. Then, as a further book appeared from Arnauld's pen, he called a meeting at Saint Lazare.

Arnauld's two books were dangerous, but far more so was Jansen's *Augustinus* on which they were founded. Its theology had been questioned already by many in Paris, and it had even earned a mild condemnation from the Vatican. Now Vincent and a number of French theologians arranged to take from it five propositions—all of which they judged to be heretical—and send them to the Pope. They did so with the request that he would declare " clearly and distinctly " what was to be done about a work which had won now so much notoriety. All ecclesiastical Paris waited then with eagerness for a pronouncement. It was long delayed, but when it came at last, it was in the form of a condemnation of the propositions so clear and forcible that there could be no evading it. A long-drawn-out battle seemed now to be at an end. The victory lay with Vincent and all the many others who had helped to bring it about, and Vincent was full of deepest thankfulness.

It was during the June of 1653 that the Bull of Condemnation reached Paris. " The Bull," Vincent wrote, " reached this city on the feast of St. Peter, and having been presented to the King and Queen, their Majesties most gladly received it, while his Eminence, the Cardinal, promised to see that it is carried out. All Paris trembled with joy at the news, at least those on the right side, and the others are showing signs that that they are willing to submit. It is hoped that all will acquiesce."

Such hopes, however, were destined only to be partially realised, the new doctrines having taken so strong a hold upon so many. But Vincent's happiness through that summer continued, and we find him asking all those theologians or heads of religious houses in Paris, who had been most eager in their condemnation of Arnauld, to abstain from any public manifestations of delight in the Pope's decision. He asked them also to treat with " friendliness, charity and respect " their defeated opponents. Conduct, however, of this order was too much to ask from the Jesuits, who had been bitterly attacked by Arnauld, and who now counter-attacked him with a delight, not wholly untinged by venom.

The unseemly warfare, which Vincent had hoped was ended, was still to go on regaling Paris. For Arnauld's voice being silenced, another defender of St. Cyran and of Jansen— and a far more brilliant one—arose in the person of Blaise Pascal, just beginning to be known as one of the great mathematicians of the age. No long book in defence of the new doctrines was asked of him, but only a pamphlet to be sold in the streets of Paris.

Pascal hesitated at first, then was inspired to express what he wanted to say in the form of a letter. This purported to be written by a young gentleman from the provinces, who, arriving in Paris and knowing little of the fight being waged, starts off with puckish delight to question all engaged in it. *A Letter to a Provincial by one of His Friends* was how this pamphlet was named, and the early hours of January 27, 1656, saw its sale in the streets of Paris. And that sale was enormous, for the letter was so original, so witty, so brilliantly written that an unprecedented sensation was created by it. Mazarin was delighted with it. The Lord Chancellor was so much excited by it that he had to be bled seven times to ward off a fit of apoplexy. Theologians, men of the Court, great ladies, all were agog with interest, and the same interest greeted the subsequent letters which presently appeared, and which are known to history as *The Provincial Letters*.

But brilliant, delightful, provocative though they were, they could make no difference to the protagonists, the works of whose leaders the Pope had condemned. To his ruling all who wished to remain in the Church must submit, a fact which brought great anguish to Mère Angélique and her community, who still loved and revered St. Cyran. Her history at this time, however, and that of her convent, Vincent never touched, for he had ceased to be a member of the Council of Conscience even before *The Provincial Letters* appeared.

No further public part in the controversy was demanded of him then, and he offered none. He never ceased to combat, however, any manifestations of the heresy with which he might come in contact, notably amongst his own missioners, quite a number of whom did succumb to its subtle power. Discussion of the subject was forbidden at Saint Lazare, and any of its members who refused to accept the Pope's ruling were banished forthwith from the Company. Vincent lost fourteen men in all, and it would be difficult to estimate how much he minded their loss. But his decision once made regarding them, he would never be moved from it. Part of the Rule of his Company stated, " It is one of the principal points of our missions to inspire others to receive the Sacraments of Penance and of the Eucharist frequently and worthily. It is fitting, therefore, that we go beyond others and give the example in this matter. So we will endeavour to attain to greater perfection in each, and that order may be maintained in all things, every priest shall confess twice (or once at the very least) every week, and shall celebrate Holy Mass every day."

The Jansenists always saw Vincent as their most merciless opponent and hated him as such ; but he would not have been true to himself if he had behaved towards them in any other way than that of extreme severity. For he saw them as shutting the door against the very means of that salvation which it was the greatest longing of his life to bring to all. He was ready to go to any lengths to keep the Sacraments within the reach of the people. He, who was usually so kindly, so gentle, so full of understanding showed no kindliness when faced with Jansenism. "As St. Ignatius and his Society were raised by God to combat Luther and Calvin," it was said, " so were Vincent de Paul and his Company raised up for the battle against Jansenism."

It was a battle which was to last even beyond his death, and one which perhaps has not been wholly won as yet.

CHAPTER XI

The War of the Fronde

IT was only in 1648—when the Jansenist controversy
was still at its height, the Bull condemning it having not yet
arrived—that the terrible Thirty Years' War came to an end.
Peace was signed then at Westphalia, all the warring powers,
save Spain, laying down their arms. Alsace was ceded to
France, who found herself thus in a better position than she
had been for many years, and it might have been thought
that a period of rest, of recuperation, perhaps of prosperity
would now be hers. But such was not to be. For even before
hostilities abroad had ceased, a civil war had broken out in
her own country, one which was to be accounted amongst
the most bitter of her history, by reason of its stupidity, its
uselessness, and the cruel callousness of its leaders. Those
leaders were mostly members of the Court, each fighting for
his own hand, and all of them careless of how much suffering
their battles, sieges, constant marching to and fro were doing
to an agricultural country and to peasantry and others of the
poor. Known as the Fronde, and so named because of its
resemblance to a game played by the children of Paris in the
streets, the Court looked upon it mostly as a mere diversion
in a boring existence. A maze of unbelievable intrigue surrounded it, while numbers of women played a prominent part
in its confused and miserable history. A redress of prevailing
grievances, an ever-growing hatred of Mazarin, and factional
contests amongst various nobles opposed to Mazarin's policy
were the main causes of hostilities which broke out in the
capital during the summer of 1648. A tax had been levied
three months previously on members of the Paris Parlement,
a municipal body without any constitutional power. Payment

of this tax was refused and, as feeling rose high, hatred of Mazarin attained to fever-heat.

Mazarin himself was at this time a man of forty-two, and at the height of his power. Still handsome, his charm undimmed, and still able to dominate the Queen, his figure was well known in countries beyond France, in which countries his astuteness and diplomacy were appreciated far more than in the country of his adoption. There the enmity he had won from the Court was based largely on the power which he, as a foreigner, wielded, while the middle-class and the very poor saw him as the author of the merciless taxation levelled against them. Stories of his fantastic wealth were noised abroad and lost nothing in the telling. He was reported to be a collector of diamonds, which report was true. His palace, adjoining the gardens of the Palais Royal, was obviously one of the loveliest in France. His stables there and his horses—the latter always bought in England—were the wonder of all who saw them.

And his wealth was certainly great. He was a lucky gambler and speculator. He had no conscience, as we have seen, about accepting large sums of money for abbeys, bishoprics and benefices. He had no conscience about accepting money from any person or any source, and having acquired it, he spent it lavishly, and yet not always foolishly. For there was a real love and appreciation of beauty and also of learning in this hot-blooded, bold Sicilian. The French Court has had many vulgar leaders of it, but he was never vulgar. And he liked to share his treasures. Thus, his collection of books, which soon came to be regarded as amongst the finest in the world, and which numbered over forty thousand volumes, he opened to the public daily. *Entrez tous qui veulent lire, entrez!* was written over the entrance to it.

His collection of pictures too, his jewels, his numberless *objets d'art* gave him increased delight because of the delight of others in them. But there was none in the capital who loved them with the extraordinary passion of love he gave them, and the story of him as a dying man going round his galleries to bid farewell to them is probably true. "*Il faut quitter tout cela!*", so he whispered as, dressed in a scarlet furred gown and leaning on a stick, he paused before each one.

These and his jewels were his heaven. And it was a heaven which was known to all in Paris, and which won no sympathy from harassed townspeople, from members of the Parlement and others.

Riots started in the capital during the August of 1648, and what the Court regarded at first as only " a blaze of straw " became in a moment a frightening conflagration. Barricades appeared without warning in the streets, and some of the mob-leaders being arrested, the temper of the people grew so ugly that it was thought advisable for the Queen and her son to leave the capital. This, accordingly, they did, but only to be summoned back almost at once. A conciliatory attitude was then adopted towards the rebels, whose leaders were pardoned. The power of Mazarin, it was announced, should be curtailed. Other promises besides were made and all seemed well. The war of the Fronde, all thought, was finished, but actually it was only the first act of it on which the curtain had just fallen, and fallen only for a short while.

It was October when the Queen returned to Paris, and through the three months which followed, grumblings continued in the capital, where the Queen and her counsellors had ruled with absolute supremacy before. Now the people were beginning to realise, as they never had hitherto, that they had some power, and they were resolved to use it.

Neither Queen nor Cardinal, however, would brook interference in their conduct and, considerably annoyed by this hostility of a usually submissive people, they presently took drastic steps to crush it. Their plan was bold. They would leave Paris in secret, taking the young King with them, and the city should then be besieged by royalist troops, who would encircle it, and reduce its inhabitants to starvation and eventual submission.

At midnight of January 5–6, 1649, the escape was carried out, its manner bearing remarkable resemblance to that of another future midnight escape from Paris of another Queen of France and her little son. But whereas Marie Antoinette's attempt to get away from the capital would end in such bitter failure at Varennes, that of Anne of Austria was destined to succeed. Anne had Mazarin with his keen brain to counsel her. Marie Antoinette had no such guide.

It was at three o'clock on the morning of January 6 that the Queen and the King crept out of the Palais Royal, and wrapped in heavy furs, entered a waiting coach which drove them through the sleeping streets of Paris to the palace of Saint Germain, a few miles outside the capital. Another followed in which sat Mazarin, who had spent many hours previously in putting away his treasures. Saint Germain was found to be empty, cold and bare, it being the custom at this time for the Court to bring all its own furniture with it when it moved about, besides its own food and servants. None of these were there to greet the royal party, whose members were thus obliged to sleep on straw with no bedclothes covering them. The cold then and later was intense.

Meanwhile, Paris had awakened to find itself a beleaguered city. The Palais Royal was empty, and beyond the city was an army commanded by the greatest military leader of the day—Condé, son to that member of the Council of Conscience, who had had so great a respect for Vincent. The encircling army had already stopped all supplies to the city, yet, the first moments of consternation passed, the fighting spirit of the people was roused and a call to arms sounded, while food was immediately requisitioned, including the vast stores held at Saint Lazare.

It was a mixed crowd which chattered now excitedly about the corners of the streets, or behind the windows of the shops, or in the great houses. For not only disgruntled members of the Parlement and poor townspeople composed it, but also a number of nobles. And with the nobles were their wives and mistresses, who found themselves all at once plunged into a drama, which was to them most wonderfully exciting. Excitement, indeed, was the prevailing note in the city during that morning.

But as days wore on and cold grew more intense and food more scarce, excitement began to dwindle, and dwindled still further when rumours of all that was happening to the people outside Paris reached those within the city. Most merciless treatment was being meted to the peasants there by Condé's troops.

Condé was young. He was not yet thirty; yet fame was already his. Tall, with keen blue eyes, long, dark, floating hair, large, eagle nose, he was careless in his dress, careless in his manner, confident of his power and position, for being first Prince of the blood, he was not far distant from the throne. Power was his passion, and to attain it he was ready to go to any lengths, even to playing the part of traitor, as his later conduct was to show. His nature had always been marked by a streak of cruelty, which now became manifested to a hideous degree. Even as early as January 7, the day after the Queen's escape, Mére Angèlique could write thus of his troops from the Convent of Port Royal of the Fields, a spot which she still quite often visited:

" This poor district is in a horrible condition. Everything has been plundered. All the horses are gone; everything has been stolen." And a few days later she writes of peasants sleeping out in woods—and this in the depths of winter—to avoid being beaten to death by Condé's soldiery, " the cruellest troops in the whole world."

Such conditions, bad then, were bound to grow much worse. Paris became every day more lifeless. Excitement was gone, or reigned only amongst the inconsequent few. No coaches were now to be seen in the streets. No posts arrived, food was scarce, while more and more the personal rivalries of the so-called leaders were gaining the upper hand. What was to be done?

The question was often asked of Vincent, who, clear-eyed as he always was, saw this war thus sprung upon the country as so senseless that a wise leader should be able to end it quickly; but there was no wise leader in the capital. It seemed to him then that it was for him to start negotiations of some kind. Mazarin, he saw, as the chief cause of all the evil. With Mazarin gone, peace might come, and surely when there was so much at stake, his dismissal should not be difficult.

Thus he argued, and knowing that he himself had influence with the Queen, he resolved to go out to Saint Germain and talk to her. Judging her by himself, he thought it would be easy to convince her that a personal feeling for her minister must not weigh against the death and suffering of countless innocent people. He knew little of either Queen or Cardinal. So with great secrecy he started forth from Saint Lazare during the night of January 14 on a journey which was fraught with danger. He was accompanied only by his secretary, and the two rode heavily cloaked, for travellers at night were regarded with suspicion. Indeed, the two would have been arrested at Clichy, which they reached at dawn, if Vincent had not been recognised by one of the guards as the latter's one-time parish priest. He was allowed to proceed then; but another even greater danger was awaiting him at Neuilly a little further on. There the Seine had risen so high that it covered a portion of the bridge, and he and his companion had to plunge into the water to reach the opposite side.

It was ten o'clock in the morning before he arrived at Saint Germain, where, tired, wet and cold, he was immediately ushered into the presence of the Queen. He remained with her an hour, then was led to the apartments of the Cardinal, with whom he pleaded, as with the Queen, to end the war. "Throw yourself into the sea," he is reported to have said to the Cardinal, "so that the storm may be appeased." Mazarin listened, quite unmoved, and it must have been small surprise to Vincent to learn the next morning that his peace proposals had been refused at the council meeting which then was held.

He remained at the palace for two more days, then sorrow-fully departed. He had failed, just as he had failed on another similar occasion when he had gone to Richelieu to stop another war. And the fault lay with him, he was convinced, for he had been so much moved that he had spoken with a harshness ill-befitting the occasion. "I have never succeeded when I have spoken with the faintest suspicion of hardness," he said. "One must be ever on one's guard not to embitter the heart, if one wishes to move the mind."

He was given a passport back to Paris, but he did not use it, for it would have been unwise to return to the capital at the moment. There his visit to the Court would have been interpreted as a move to betray the city. Distrust and suspicion were so much in the air that even his word would not have been taken that he had gone to Queen and Cardinal only to negotiate.

So he turned away instead to visit some of the country places where members of his Congregation were established, though it was assuredly no time to visit them with the winter at its hardest and the country at war. He set forth undeterred, however, and presently reached a little place called Fréneville where was a farm which supplied Saint Lazare with much of its food. He had thought to stay there for only a few days, but heavy falls of snow obliged him to remain for over a month, and it is a proof of his hardiness that he at his age—he was nearly seventy—should have survived the conditions which he found. He had for fuel only logs of damp green wood and for food mouldy bread and fruit. Some Sisters of Charity close by, however, at length provided him with some of their own brown bread and apples. He preached every Sunday in the village church and shared all the work of the missioners in charge of the scattered little parish.

News from Paris often reached him and it was never good. Saint Lazare had been invaded and any remaining stores of corn and flour commandeered. Then the building itself was taken over, its occupants ordered to leave, while six hundred soldiers were quartered in it. Following a protest to the Parlement, however, from the Superior whom Vincent had left behind, the soldiers were turned out and its previous inhabitants restored. But with its stores of food gone, together with its stores of fuel, its usefulness in a starving city had ceased, and a decision was made to empty it. It was left then with only the Superior and a few priests and brothers, besides a handful of students to mount guard over it.

Vincent, meanwhile, continued his country travels, riding through snow, and flooded, devastated areas. He came near death several times, as his horse stumbled over frozen streams and rivers. He would spend nights in uncomfortable inns and cottages. But spring was coming. Travelling would soon be easier and his journeys were important, even though they were beginning by this time to take their toll of him. Disregarding all weakness, however, he decided to ride southwards to Marseilles, where there were some missioners whom he would like to visit. And he was just about to set out thither when a message came to him from the Queen asking him to return to Paris.

Peace had lately been signed between the belligerents; though, to any possessing any real knowledge of the situation, it was quite obviously no real peace. The siege might be lifted, fighting had ceased, and food was reaching the capital ; but conditions otherwise were grave. For an enmity which had always existed between Condé and Mazarin—the two greatest men of the day—had now risen to such a pitch that it constituted a pressing danger to all.

Vincent was staying at a little place called Richelieu on the Loire, not far from Chinon, when the Queen's request came to him. He received it as a command and reluctantly laid aside his plan to go to Marseilles, even though he was feeling so ill by now that it was a plan which he could hardly have carried out. " I do not see how I can do the will of God," he wrote to the Superior of the house he had designed to visit, " if I do not obey the Queen. For I have always believed and taught that the will of princes must not be set aside."

The will of the Queen, nevertheless, had to be set aside for some days, " a tiny, little fever " from which Vincent had unwillingly admitted he was suffering, having become sufficiently bad for him to be unable to mount a horse. News of his illness reaching Saint Lazare, the brother infirmarian there was sent to Richelieu to nurse him. His arrival was not welcomed by Vincent. " My illness is not severe," Vincent remarked coldly. " Was it necessary to send to me a brother from Saint Lazare ? " Then, swiftly penitent for words which might have caused the brother pain, he asked forgiveness.

But he was to be further and even more deeply irritated the next day when a carriage appeared to take him back to Paris. It was drawn by two fine horses and driven by the coachman of the Duchesse d'Aiguillon, a niece of Richelieu's, and one of the Ladies of Charity. Actually, the carriage was his own, a gift from the Ladies of Charity, but he had always refused to use it. Why should he drive about in state, he asked, he, the son of a poor peasant ? But the carriage was there and he was ill, and only the greatest kindness had prompted its despatch. The Duchesse, indeed, would be hurt if he refused it, so as soon as he was better, he stepped inside it. But arrived at Saint Lazare, he banished it at once to the stables, while returning the horses to the Duchesse. She sent them back, however, and in the end—though only with the help of the Archbishop of Paris as well as of the Queen—the carriage was taken from the stable and put into

use. "My shame," Vincent called it, "my disgrace," and
he exacted revenge for the gift by picking up any poor persons
whom he passed on his travels and taking them to their
destinations. The horses also "had to suffer humiliation,"
for when not in the carriage, they were yoked to ploughs and
carts.

It was a different Saint Lazare he found on his return from
that which he had left. It was empty, cold and dead, while
an evil spirit was abroad in Paris, which the Queen's return
in August did little to dispel. Condé was there and, with his
insatiable lust for power, was the leader of the younger nobles
of the Court, men who had neither sympathy for the people,
nor respect for their rulers. Turbulent, insolent, intriguing,
they and the women who influenced them, "the beautiful,
witty, dissolute duchesses," designed to rule Paris and even
France itself. Mazarin, who faced this motley throng, had
more elements of greatness in him than any of them. But he
was hated by all except the Queen.

Now as the power of Condé increased each day, the Queen
grew more and more afraid of him, until at last—prompted
by Mazarin—she ordered his arrest. He was captured,
accordingly, and sent during the January of 1650 to the prison
of Vincennes. For a year he remained a captive, while risings
in his favour all over the country provoked most bitter fighting.
Then, as this grew fiercer, Mazarin advised the Queen to
release him, while promising himself to go into voluntary
exile. He left Paris on the night of February 6, 1651, "by
the light of the moon" for the palace of Saint Germain, and
Condé returned to the capital.

He did so with soaring hopes that he would soon be ruler
of both Queen and Court; but such hopes were quickly
dashed. His own almost unbelievable arrogance was his
undoing, together with the intrigues against him of the many
nobles in the capital, all intent on gaining position for themselves. At last, fearful of another arrest, he fled the city, and
baffled and disappointed, sold himself to Spain, an enemy
against whom he had fought so many brilliant battles in the
past. For he must have Paris, no matter what the price, and
during the following summer he marched upon it, leader of
a large and well-trained army. And it fell to him, though only

as the result of help given to him by a woman there, first cousin to the King, and known to history as *La Grande Mademoiselle*. She turned the guns of the Bastille on the royal army in the city and so won victory for Condé and his men.

It was during the July of 1652 that this happened, and through the succeeding burning weeks of summer, Paris echoed to the sound of guns. The Queen and the young King had hurriedly left the capital, which was, indeed, no safe place for anybody. " I am preparing for death," Louise de Marillac wrote once to Vincent, and she was not ashamed to add that she felt her heart " jumping " each time she heard in the streets the cry of *Aux Armes!* Complete anarchy was reigning. On the night of July 1–2 some of Condé's army broke into part of Saint Lazare, carrying off with them " everything that took their fancy." A passing Swiss soldier, however, and another set upon them and compelled them to abandon their booty. " But as things are rapidly growing worse," Vincent wrote three days after, " we have been advised to keep some armed men on the premises. In fact, we have had them with us this very night and I remained up with them."

The Hôtel de Ville had been burned down, and several councillors of the city murdered. Food was scarce and each day saw numbers of refugees pouring into the capital. A few days before Condé's entry Vincent had written thus to some Sisters of Charity in the country—" We would send a Sister to help you, if that were possible, but you know the dangerous state of the roads, while things are so bad in Paris that Mademoiselle Le Gras has not enough Sisters to help the sick and the poor refugees. Our Sisters of Saint Paul's are dispensing soup every day to nearly eight thousand persons, without counting the sixty or eighty invalids they have always on their hands."

But if the condition of Paris was bad, that of the surrounding districts was much worse. The tales of those who had managed to escape from them were terrible to hear, and Vincent, who heard more of them than anybody else—from his missioners as well as from the people themselves—was moved once more to take swift action. This time appeal to Mazarin would be of no avail, nor yet to the Queen. He would approach instead the man who should have the greatest influence of any in the world—the Pope himself.

So on August 16, 1652 he wrote to him, a long letter which may still be seen in the archives of the Vatican. Simply, yet dramatically he describes in it " the lamentable state of France " with its royal house divided, towns and villages and cities destroyed, and peasants " unable to reap what they have sown or to sow for their future needs."

" The soldiers indulge with impunity in the worst excesses, and expose the people not only to rapine and plunder, but also to murder and all forms of torture. Such country-folk as have not been smitten with the sword are almost all dying of hunger. Priests, whom the soldiers do not spare any more than they do the rest of the people, are inhumanly and cruelly treated, tortured and put to death. Virgins are dishonoured, and even nuns themselves exposed to their libertinism and rage. Churches are profaned, pillaged and destroyed, while those that remain standing are for the most part abandoned by their pastors, so that the people are almost deprived of the Sacraments, Mass and all spiritual helps and succour.

" Lastly, a thing most horrible to think of, and still more horrible to utter, the most holy Sacrament of the Body of Our Lord is treated with the greatest indignity even by Catholics, for in order to plunder the sacred vessels, they cast down and trample upon the Holy Eucharist. What then is the conduct of heretics, who do not believe in these mysteries ? I neither dare, nor can express it. It is but a small thing to hear and speak of such things ; they must be seen with one's eyes and experienced.

" Indeed, most holy Father, there remains no other remedy for our ills save that which can come from the paternal solici-tude, affection and authority of your Holiness. May your Holiness deign to realise our desires. Over and over again I implore your Holiness to do so, pleading with you the mercy of Jesus Christ, whose place you hold, and whose Person you represent upon this earth. I implore also for myself the apostolic benediction.

" Your Holiness's most humble, obedient, and devoted
          servant and son in Jesus Christ,
                              " Vincent de Paul."

The letter was despatched and an answer eagerly awaited ; but no answer came. And meanwhile, Paris under the domination of Condé was enduring a harsher and more cruel rule than had ever been her lot under any of her kings. Condé ruled as a despot and a ruthless one. Determined to subdue Paris, he was doing so, but at the expense not only of his own fame, but of his cause. A burning hatred for him now smouldered in the hearts of all, and eyes began to turn longingly towards the exiled Queen. She must come back to them, it was whispered. At any price, she must return. She, who might be often foolish, was never cruel, and she would bring with her, if she came, her son, who was the rightful King, and who had won already a deep affection in the hearts of all who had ever seen him. Soon it was said that a welcome would even be accorded to Mazarin.

Such were the underground mutterings which Vincent was the first to hear, and hearing them, he approached Mazarin in his exile with news of them. For the Cardinal might not know, he thought, of the changed face of Paris, and if he were to be informed, he might use his great influence to bring about what the people now so greatly wanted, and thus end quickly the suffering which was deepening and increasing on all sides.

"I summon up courage to write to your Eminence," Vincent's letter, dated September 11, 1652, begins, "to tell your Eminence that I now see France returning to its former condition and calling out with might and main for the King and Queen. And because of this, I think your Eminence would perform an act worthy of the kindness of an adviser to the King and Queen, if you were to ask them to return and take possession of their city and the hearts of Paris." The letter, which is very long, goes on then to enumerate a number of objections which might be raised to such a course of conduct, all of which Vincent meets with the shrewd commonsense which was part of him. And the letter takes for granted that the Cardinal must accompany the Queen and the young King whom, it seemed, were quite literally incapable of doing without him. And whether he came before or after their arrival did not vitally matter.

"It does not matter very much whether your Eminence returns before or after the King, provided you do return, and that once His Majesty is re-established in Paris, His Majesty can recall you at his pleasure." Then with a quiet courage, which is astonishing, the old mission priest advises the mighty Cardinal on his future administration. No policy of revenge, he asks, should be his, while he implores that free access may be allowed to the King from all sides, and that the Court may not be peopled by strangers, members of the Cardinal's own domestic household. " For, it is very much to be feared, my Lord, that if such procedure continues, the opportunity may be lost and the hatred of the people rise and turn to rage. On the other hand, if your Eminence advises the King to come to Paris and receive the loyal greetings of his people, you will win the hearts of all those in the kingdom, who are well aware of your influence with the King and Queen, and all will attribute the favour to your Eminence.

" I have summoned up courage, my Lord, to put this before you in the hope that you will not find it amiss, especially when your Eminence learns that I have not mentioned the matter to anyone in the world, save a servant of your Eminence, to whom I have done myself the honour of writing, and that I shall live and die in the obedience due to your Eminence, to whom Our Lord has committed me in a special manner. And hence I assure you, my Lord, that I am your most humble, faithful and obedient servant,

" Vincent de Paul."

But, as always, when Vincent took a hand in politics he failed, and an icy reply from Mazarin to the effect that Vincent being no longer a member of the Council of Conscience, his advice was superfluous, was the sole answer to a letter which must have cost him much to write. And actually, it was unnecessary, for those in authority had seen the situation no less clearly than had Vincent. Requests for peace had already come from Paris. Condé's power was gone and the way well paved for the King's return. He, advised by Mazarin, proclaimed a general amnesty, which he kept, and his entry into the capital was a triumphant one. It took place in October and was marked by scenes of wild enthusiasm. Mazarin did not accompany him.

Thus the war of the Fronde came to an end at last, leaving

a greatly impoverished country, but a monarchy which was in a stronger position than it had ever been before. People, members of the Parlement, nobles had all alike shown themselves so incapable of rule that even that of Mazarin was coveted. And in fact, when he did return to the capital at the beginning of the following year, he was greeted with something the same delight as that which had been accorded to the King.

CHAPTER XII

Aftermath of War

THE war might be over, but not so its results, and the years immediately following it were amongst the busiest of Vincent's life. They were spent almost entirely in Paris— the heart of the country, as Saint Lazare was the heart of the city. To Saint Lazare, as always, came hundreds each day to be fed, or to plead for refuge. Yet still retreats were held beneath its roof, still Vincent instructed little companies of the Sisters of Charity each week, and helped with advice those who were working amongst foundlings and prisoners. Still he guided Ladies of Charity and numbers of others, while acting as Father Superior to his Congregation of Mission Priests, and still he somehow found time to spend hours of prayer in the chapel of Saint Lazare. Indeed, he would have said himself that without those hours of stillness he could have accomplished nothing.

Noise and confusion, poverty and suffering might be reigning in the thronging streets outside, but in Saint Lazare was quietness. All who crossed its threshold were aware immediately that here was a house of prayer. And more prayer was being made at this time within its walls than at any other period of its history, Vincent having ordered, even before peace came, that specific times should be given up to pleading for the suffering people round. "Whilst they are suffering and battling against extreme privation, and all the other miseries they endure," he said, "it behoves us to act like Moses, and following his example, lift up our hands increasingly to heaven on their behalf. We should be their intercessors with the Divine Mercy." A daily Mass for peace was said, while penance was enjoined as well, three members of the Congregation being deputed to fast rigorously each day.

He had started to give missions to refugees a few months before the King's return to Paris, and this even in spite of the fact that one of the rules of the Congregation was that missions should be held only in country places. Those country places, however, were now so devastated that they were uninhabitable, and it was their occupants who were at his doors, and whose souls he desired so much to save. " We are bound to go and serve the refugees in the country when they are there, and now that they have come to us, driven away by the rigour of war, it would seem that we are even more strictly bound to labour for their salvation in the afflicted conditions in which they are." Two retreats were given during the June of 1652 in one of which he took part himself.

Priests and nuns were often to be found amongst the refugees, and to these he always gave most special help. The priests would be lodged at once in Saint Lazare, and he had presently rented a small house where nuns could stay under the care of some of those Visitation Sisters whom Francis de Sales had left to his guidance long years before.

These were certainly in need of help, but they were well-off by comparison with the many who arrived in the capital so ill that they reached it only to die. The Hôtel Dieu was soon so full that all had to sleep on straw mattresses, while more numbers than ever were crowded into the available beds. It was estimated that more than a hundred died each day within its walls, and there were other hospitals besides in the city where much the same conditions prevailed. The Ladies of Charity were still constant visitors at the Hôtel Dieu, and now many of them started to take some of the sick into their own homes.

Indeed, as the tale of suffering mounted, and as the people of Paris realised more and more how great it was—as much outside its gates as within them—their hearts were moved to an almost boundless generosity, which increased after peace came, bringing with it the return of the King and Queen.

All priests were told then that they must help with collections in their churches, and with meetings to provide relief for these afflicted people. And organisations quickly sprang to life. Soon the presbyteries of all the Paris churches were turned into store-houses where gifts of every description could be left. These comprised anything from food and medicine and clothes to books, workmen's tools, devotional objects, all of which would be taken each day to central clearing-houses for distribution. It was estimated that during the first three months following the signing of peace about six thousand pounds of meat were given away weekly, besides several thousand eggs, and other provisions on a similar scale.

Then groups of people banded themselves together and drove little carts from house to house collecting all they could. The Company of Butchers, the Hosiers' Company, and other civic organisations gave most generously, but even more so did the Ladies of Charity, who gave their services, as we have seen, and also jewellery and money. One sent a dress she had been wearing " to clothe," as she said, " the members of Jesus Christ." At Court the maids-of-honour started a Confraternity of Charity for the help of the distressed, and many a lovely *objet d'art* and piece of crested silver was found at one or other place of collection. The very poor also were not to be outdone in generosity. They would bring little presents of food which they had hoarded for themselves, and which they could ill spare. One woman arrived at a clearing centre one day with a bundle of clothes beneath her arm which she deposited, then took off her shoes and departed barefooted. A bystander remarked that surely she had more need to receive than to give, to which she replied that she had given of her best.

The whole of Paris was now united in an effort to do everything possible—Jesuits and Jansenists, lawyers, magistrates, members of the Court, and not least the ever kindly Queen. The Jansenists had been amongst the first to be moved by compassion and Mère Angélique, whether from Paris or from her convent in the country, was as practical in her efforts to combat the prevailing misery as Vincent de Paul himself. The Jesuits issued little pamphlets of instruction to all who desired to help. " Visitors are directed to find out the particular reason why the family is poor. If the case is a genuine one, work should be found for the parents. Furniture stamped with a parochial mark may be lent if necessary. Creditors are to be compounded with, the daughters apprenticed, and the family, if lapsed, be induced to attend to its religious duties. Money may only be given under exceptional circumstances." Amongst the numbers of unnamed heroes of the time were doctors, who " toiled day and night for the magnificent wage of fifteen sous a day." Many, discarding even such " magnificent wage," worked for nothing, and not a few gave their lives for those whom they had been called to help. Any appeal for volunteers met with a ready response, and a Huguenot minister would sometimes be found working side by side with a Catholic priest. The enthusiasm of the moment, it has been said, " spread beyond class and sect and became as Catholic as love itself."

During the February of 1653 Mazarin returned to Paris, which he had not seen for many months. It was a different city from that which he had left. Poverty was everywhere and not only in the streets ; it had reached to palaces as well. The crown jewels had been sold, and a less glittering throng than he remembered peopled the rooms and galleries of the Palais Royal, while his own palace had been despoiled of all the treasures he had been unable to take away. Numbers of them, however, he managed to buy back. The magistrates and members of that Parlement, which had revolted against his rule, now came to offer him their homage. The princes and principal nobles, who had played so sorry a part in recent events, came too. He, like the King, was in a stronger position than had ever been his before.

He and Vincent do not seem to have met during these early months of his return, and we do not hear of Vincent making any visits to the Palais Royal, though he was presently in correspondence with the Queen about a vast project which she was anxious to set on foot. It was concerned with the problem of mendicancy.

Long years before, when Vincent first became a mission-priest, he had been brought face to face with the question at that small provincial town of Mâcon. He had dealt with it successfully there, but here in Paris it confronted him on a far bigger scale. The Thirty Years' War had first brought such vast hordes of beggars to the capital that they had become

a definite menace, spreading "fear and terror by their mis-
demeanours." Now the war of the Fronde had brought far
more. The streets were not safe from them by day or by
night. Civic authorities, as well as religious organisations,
met frequently to discuss the evil and find a remedy, "the
desolate state of the souls of these mendicants" being in that
age, when religion was so closely woven into daily life, one of
the things which distressed authorities almost as much as
any other.

Many charitable institutions—Saint Lazare amongst them—
helped with the distribution of food to them each week; but
such generosity left the real root of the evil untouched, as
Vincent was well aware. Yet he felt no call to take any definite
steps to combat it until in 1647—two years before the outbreak
of the Fronde—when a man came to him one day, bringing
with him the gift of a large sum of money. This, he told
Vincent, he could use in any way he wished, and at once
Vincent thought of the homeless beggars, whose plight was
seldom absent from his mind. Here, it seemed, was a chance
to put into practice a project which actually he had been
considering for some time.

Quite near Saint Lazare was a house called *Le Nom de Jésus*,
and this Vincent had lately acquired. What could be better
than to turn it into a home for the old and poor? The donor
of the money, who desired to be anonymous, and who has
always remained so, agreed, and Vincent immediately wrote
to ask the advice of Louise de Marillac, whose opinion on
such subjects he always valued more than that of any other.
The building was large enough to accommodate about forty
people—twenty men and twenty women. Louise was deeply
interested in the idea and wrote Vincent a letter so clear and
practical that we realise afresh how wise Vincent was to lean
upon her judgment.

She was in favour of the scheme, but urged that the forty
chosen people should not be beggars but "decent poor folk,"
and that they should be given besides a home, definite work
to do in it, or a definite training in such work if this were
necessary. Thus the first group of inmates, she felt strongly,
should contain amongst its numbers several capable of teaching
a trade—a shoemaker, a silkweaver, a cobbler, a lacemaker,

a dressmaker. For not only would sale of the finished work, which the old people would be thus enabled to do, help in the maintenance of the house, but the doing of it would make for their happiness and self-respect. A fourth part of any profits which accrued should be given to them. " Having a sufficient number of good workmen," Louise wrote, " to make a good start and to carry on the work, we should not worry about the expense which must be incurred for tools, implements and materials. Divine Providence will not fail us in any respect, though we must fully make up our minds that there will be very little profit the first year." Her advice was taken, and it was then arranged that the administration of the house should rest with Vincent and two others, both to be citizens of Paris, while one of Vincent's missioners was to be responsible for the religious side of the work.

Plans were then made for a speedy opening of the house, but first many structural alterations must be made in it, and before these could be completed the Fronde came to put an end to all such work. The house was not opened until March, 1653, a month after Mazarin's return to Paris. On the opening day Vincent and Louise welcomed the inmates, who appeared most gaily dressed in clothes which had been provided for them. Saint Lazare was so close to the house that Vincent could often visit it, while Louise, who kept all the accounts of it, was also a frequent visitor.

And the project was successful, even though grumblings were heard at first amongst the old people because of a rule which prevented them from going out and coming in at will. " But as they settled down," writes a contemporary, " a marvellous peace and unity were found amongst them. Grumbling and backbiting were banished with other vices. The poor busied themselves with their little employments and acquitted themselves of all the religious duties appropriate to their state. It was, in fine, a little replica of the early Christians."

The waiting list for it was soon so long and the whole scheme so successful that it was small wonder many should have been convinced—and notably the Ladies of Charity— that if Vincent were to be given power and funds on a large scale, he would be able to go a long way towards solving the problem of mendicancy which the recent war of the Fronde had now made more urgent. And suggestions concerning it were presently made to him.

On the further bank of the river was an enormous building known as La Saltpêtrière, which was the property of the crown. The Ladies of Charity now asked the Queen if she would hand it over to Vincent to be made into a refuge for vagrants. She consented at once. She was still fond of Vincent, and being no business woman, she thought that this colossal work would be quite easy. The Ladies of Charity, who were no business women either, thought the same, and with the Queen's consent obtained, they were eager to hurry matters forward with as much speed as possible. But Vincent, who was a business man, and a particularly astute one, held back, not only because of his constitutional slowness but because of the magnitude of the task.

The Saltpêtrière was of such proportions that it was capable of holding many thousands of people. The conversion of it then into a refuge for the poor could not be undertaken lightly. It must be pondered over and considered with the utmost care—a fact which the Ladies of Charity found impossible to understand. More and more as Vincent waited and considered did their impatience grow, Vincent's methods of dealing with such impatience having the opposite effect of that desired. The Ladies would be reminded of the slowness of God, of Noah's ark which took a hundred years to build, and of the Children of Israel who had to wait forty years before entering the Promised Land. " God does not hasten His works. He does all things in their time. It is not expedient to wish to do everything all at once, or to think that all is lost if everybody else does not hurry along with us."

He allowed them, nevertheless, to have their way at length to the extent of permitting workmen to be installed in the building, and by the autumn a certain amount of reconstruction had been made. The Ladies must have looked on at it with growing satisfaction, when all at once a blow fell.

The civic authorities, members of the Court and others, aware of this new venture going forward, lodged a protest against it. The planning of any institution on so vast a scale, they said, must have official authority, and should be under

State, and not private control. They ordered, therefore, that all work on the Saltpêtrière should cease. They would be responsible for the whole scheme instead. And sorrowfully the Ladies of Charity had to acquiesce. They did so, however, only after considerable protest and on the advice of Vincent, who saw immediately that resistance to such an edict was impossible.

Thus the great plan, so finely and unselfishly conceived, had to be abandoned, though the large sums of money which the Ladies of Charity had already spent on it they did not demand back. Their conduct throughout was extraordinarily fine. And so was Vincent's, who said nothing, as he watched with deep misgiving the construction of something of which he could not approve.

The Saltpêtrière was ready for use by the spring of 1657, and on May 7 a notice was given out from every pulpit in Paris that its doors would be opened the following week, and that from that time begging in the capital would be regarded as a punishable offence. Beggars were to go to the Saltpêtrière, and any who refused to do so, would be taken there by force. The streets, it had been decided, were to be cleared of them at whatever cost, and cleared they were. The genuinely destitute obeyed the royal command. Some, who were quite able-bodied " resigned themselves to the necessity of work," while amongst the supposedly very ill appeared, we are told, thousands of sudden cures. " The blind recovered their sight; the maimed and the crippled the use of their limbs; the paralysed their power of movement. Never did medicine effect so many and such rapid cures as did the decree of the Parlement." But it was a sort of " medicine " of which Vincent could not approve, the idea of force being so bitterly repugnant to him. He saw poverty also, which is not in itself a crime, being treated as such, and his heart was filled with sorrow.

The reform, nevertheless, was so necessary that, imperfect though it was, it cannot be condemned. Paris had to be freed from a growing and terrifying evil, while something had to be done to keep the many thousands of genuinely destitute people from dying of hunger or exposure in the streets.

Vincent's advice was frequently asked before the opening of the building, and it was the King's special wish—the King being then a youth of nineteen—that the spiritual care of the General Hospital, as it was henceforward called, should be entrusted to Vincent's mission priests. "As we have long known the blessings which God has bestowed on the labours of the mission priests of Saint Lazare," he wrote, "it is our wish that they may assist and console the poor of the General Hospital and those other houses over which it has authority, and that they may be entrusted with the administration of the Sacraments, under the authority and jurisdiction of the Lord Archbishop of Paris."

But this command Vincent could not obey, though only because the number of priests necessary for the work was beyond his capacity to supply. He assembled, however, a band of men, selected mostly from priests who attended his Tuesday Conferences, and presenting the position to them, he won from them a promise to do all in their power to help. Vincent by this act, however, cut himself off henceforth from all administrative connection with the building, though his influence was still felt in it through the work of the Ladies of Charity, a number of whom were elected to the staff of it. They, as always, gave of their service as well as of their money.

But the new reform was unpopular, as can be imagined, with those whom it was designed to help, and many of them heaped much abuse on Vincent because of it. "Do you know what people are saying about you, Father?" a one-time beggar asked of him one day. "Please tell me," Vincent answered. "They are full of resentment against you because they think you are the cause of the poor people being shut up in the big hospital." Vincent's only reply was that he would pray for all those there.

His unpopularity was further increased when, in accordance with the new laws now framed, he was obliged to put an end to the former daily distribution of bread and soup to the very poor at the gates of Saint Lazare. The anger caused by this action was very deep. "Father, did not God command that alms should be given to the poor?" "That is quite true, my friends, but He also commanded us to obey the magistrates."

He temporarily relaxed the rule, however, as a particularly hard winter followed the opening of the General Hospital.

Whether he himself ever entered the building after its opening we do not know. It is likely, however, that he did, even though he had no authority—as we have seen—over those in power there. His own little foundation, *Le Nom de Jésus* might have been the ostensible pattern of it, food and comfort and work being amongst the things which the inmates of the General Hospital were given. But the happiness of the smaller building was absent from the vast Saltpêtrière. There, force rather than charity held sway, and fighting and riots were presently of almost ordinary occurrence. Yet the Ladies of Charity, undeterred, continued their work amongst its inhabitants, and did so even after Vincent's death, which makes us realise afresh how well they had assimilated the teaching he had given them.

Chapter XIII

Father Superior General

VINCENT'S company of mission priests numbered now some four hundred men, yet their work was so vast and far-flung that had he sent any to the General Hospital, it would have meant the relinquishment by them of something equally important already undertaken.

They had only lately become a religious order, Vincent having been for a long time opposed to the idea of any formal rule to bind them, while many men had been attracted to his Company just because they knew no vow was involved in joining it. "Everybody here has such an aversion from the religious state as is quite lamentable," Vincent wrote in 1649, and a few months later—"Dislike of the religious state is common. I find myself in great perplexity." For he was beginning to question seriously even then the advisability of a vow. His sons were mostly against the idea of taking one, while the Vatican was definitely hostile towards the foundation of a fresh religious order. There were too many, it considered, already in existence, the majority of them being of a most unedifying nature. Still Vincent pondered, then wrote thus in 1651 to one of his missioners in Rome:

"Unless we have some sort of chain to unite us to each other and collectively to God, many will join us only to gain experience and to fit themselves for public work, and will then be off. And others, who were strong in purpose at the beginning, will none the less give up at the first drawback or at the chance of a good opening in the world, there being nothing to hold them. We have only too much experience of such failures, and even now as I write, we have one man, who having been trained and schooled for thirteen or fourteen years, has just asked for funds to help him to start something else, and only waits until he has them to leave us. What remedy is there for the evil? How shall we avoid wasting the funds—given to us to help in the salvation of the poor—on people of this kind, if we have no means of holding them by some strong bond of conscience, such as a vow of perseverance?" He writes again two years later in a similar strain. "There is so much variety in our undertakings, they are so trying and so prolonged, those employed in them suffer so many rebuffs and are confronted with so much opposition, that it is hard for them to be steadfast if they are not bound to the Company. Many too are so light-minded that what they choose today, they will weary of tomorrow."

Here was the expression of a complete conviction that a vow was a necessity, and Vincent worked henceforth quietly and inexorably for recognition of its wisdom from the Vatican. Then that recognition came. The year 1655 brought a Papal Brief approving of the taking of the threefold vow by members of his Congregation, which vow might be dispensed only by the Pope and by himself as Superior General.

Vincent's delight was great. "We have received the Brief containing the approbation of our vows, thanks be to God," he wrote immediately to one of his sons. "For it is to God alone that we are indebted, since it is true that without a special guidance on His part, it would have been impossible to surmount the obstacles. May the divine goodness thereby be ever glorified."

Three months later, life vows were taken by all members of the Company then at Saint Lazare, their names being inscribed in a book which may still be seen in the mother-house of Paris. A sign and seal had thus been set to a work, which Vincent always regarded as the most important of his life. Others might see him as primarily a great religious reformer or philanthropist. He saw himself as primarily the Superior General of the Company he had founded. It was known then as the "Congregation of the Mission," a title which it bears still.

Its history had been remarkable, and still more remarkable was the continuing response its members made to the demands required of them. For it still asked of them everything and gave them back nothing seemingly in return. " Those who joined it renounced all choice in their career," it has been written of them, " all ordinary ambitions, every tie of blood. They were bound to a reality of poverty such as was rarely practised by the Religious." " He who would live in the Congregation," wrote Vincent, " must be prepared to live as a pilgrim upon earth, to sacrifice his reason for Christ's sake, to change all his habits, to mortify every passion, to seek God only, to be subject to anyone as being himself the least of all, to realise that he has come to serve and not to govern, to suffer and to labour and not to live in comfort or idleness."

Here was tremendous hardness and yet—paradoxically as it seems—only great joy resulted and was the hall-mark of the Congregation. Those years spent by Vincent at the Collège des Bons Enfants, when he was free to go off into the country to succour and to save those who were lost, he always regarded as the happiest of his life. How could they have been otherwise, since he was following then, more closely than was possible in any other way, the footsteps of the Saviour whom he loved with such a passion of devotion?

And that love he had communicated to his sons, who could never have faced what was asked of them as a matter of course had they not also possessed something of his inspiring ideal. We have seen already the sort of service demanded of them when one war after another swept over France, while those who went abroad found other equally terrible conditions. Those conditions, indeed, were more terrible than any Vincent himself had ever known, and we do not wonder as we read of them and the spirit in which they were met, how much Vincent hated the praise and also the gifts which were lavished on him personally and which he could not share with his sons. His carriage really was to him his " shame," and so were other little luxuries which, as he grew older, he was obliged to accept. But he was too big to dwell upon them, and certainly there was none in his Congregation who grudged them to him.

He won as Superior General unfailing love from those he governed. Accessible to all, the door of his room, we are told, " stood ever open to them. He welcomed them affably and listened to them attentively. Those who were about to leave

Saint Lazare to preach a mission, or who returned from one, always went to him to ask his blessing; he would then kneel to them himself and embrace them with the utmost tenderness." His presence was a stimulation to them. His understanding of them was so deep, his sympathy so true.

And yet he could be hard at times—as he was hard to the Jansenists—almost to the point of ruthlessness, and no disobedience to his commands ever went unnoticed. Thus one of his sons—who having been obliged to work on some urgent business far into the night, and having been told not to attend chapel at half-past four the next morning, nevertheless appeared—was rebuked before the whole Community for his "imprudent fervour." And another of his sons, Père de la Fosse, a fine scholar and a master of several languages, was rebuked even more severely for what Vincent considered a display of miserable pride. The man, whose humour, we cannot help feeling, was even stronger than his pride, had gone to see the performance of a play at a college near, when a message arrived asking him to change his seat. He did not want to change his seat, so pretending not to understand the request, he replied in Latin that he was quite comfortable where he was. "If he talks Latin," thought the Principal, "he must be an Irishman," and he sent someone to speak to him in Latin. A similar reply was made by Père de la Fosse in Greek. "Then he must be an ecclesiastic just arrived from Lebanon," thought the slightly bewildered Principal, and sent him a professor of rhetoric. "Go and speak to him in Greek," he said. "He may perhaps in the end understand the request." A reply came from Père de la Fosse in Hebrew and he was then allowed to remain seated where he was. The incident caused delight to those at Saint Lazare, but it caused no delight to Vincent, who having severely reprimanded Père de la Fosse, ordered him to go off at once to the college, there to apologise on his knees to the Principal for what he had done. "But history," comments the narrator of the story, "does not tell us if he used as many languages when making his apology as he had done when committing his offence."

Vincent may have been stern at times, yet nobody seems ever to have been afraid of him, and he had a special sympathy with and understanding of the lay brothers of the Congregation. Their lot in so large a community could often be very hard, though it is true that many of them were of so mean an intelligence that much patience had to be exercised in dealing with them. One who came to him once with complaints of ill-treatment was tenderly received. " You did right to let me know about this, Brother," Vincent said, " and always come to me again, for you know how well I love you." Another, complaining to him of an insult offered him by one of the domestics of the house, was received with equal gentleness, and the offending domestic was dismissed even though his work was valuable.

The same kindness was extended to all difficult members of the Congregation, whom he would try in every possible way to help. " He aimed," we are told, " at imitating the wise physician who, before abandoning all hope of his patients' cure, exhausts every remedy, and hence he employed every means in his power : prayers, admonitions and warnings. He used to recall that this was the method of Our Lord with the Apostles. ' Our Saviour did not cast off St. Peter for having denied Him thrice,' he said, ' nor even Judas, though He foresaw he would die in his sins. It is only in the last resort that we should have recourse to dismissal.' " And when dismissal had to be resorted to, he gave it with great anguish. " When I see somebody who must be sent away, I fear asking him to go far more strongly than three attacks of fever. But it has to be done, for we must be firm. He is not a skilful surgeon who only knows how to apply a plaster ; he should know how to cut and how to remove a limb when the others are threatened with injury."

A favourite method of rebuke with him was to combine it with a rebuke of himself. " You see, sir, you and I allow ourselves to be carried away by our opinions. Remember that you and I are subject to a thousand impulses of nature. You will, if you please, correct your readiness to carry out affairs, and I will endeavour to correct my easy-going ways." Then with a sudden burst of the tenderness which was so true a part of him, he writes : " I beseech you, sir, to bear with the simple way in which I address you and not to be offended by it ; but rather to act like those brave pilots, who caught in a great storm, redouble their courage, and turn the prow of their vessels towards the most furious waves of the sea."

Vincent once proudly described Saint Lazare as a "little paradise," and it is true that all who entered it were struck immediately by its prevailing happiness. Yet the discipline was at times so hard that complaints of it would be made to Vincent. He would never relax anything of the Rule, however, and refused always to change that part of it which was concerned with early rising. Members of the Congregation minded it so much that at last he wrote a long letter about it, which he ordered to be circulated to all.

"Nature," he wrote, "presumes on everything we yield to her. If we rest one day, the next she will ask for the same indulgence, while actually mind and body are the better for the regularity of sleep. Those who allow themselves much become effeminate and open the door to temptations.

"In some, however, the love of soft living will not surrender without remonstrance, and because there may be an excuse for saying that the rule of rising should not be equally binding on strong and weak, I foresee it will be urged that the weak need longer rest than others. To that the best answer is the opinion of doctors, who all agree that seven hours' sleep is enough for all sorts of people, and also the example of all religious Orders, who limit sleep to seven hours.

"So, my brother, my friend, you must get up if you are not in hospital, or have not received a special order to remain in bed; for if you have got no relief from seven hours' sleep, one or two more hours prescribed by yourself will not cure you. Unless this is the rule, we shall be forced to begin all over again, because so many will very often feel some illness, and others will pretend that they do. If we do not sleep soundly one night, nature is very well able to make up for the lack of it the next night.

"'But do you mean, sir,' I hear someone asking, 'to forbid any extra rest to those who have come off a journey or who have just completed some arduous task?' I answer, Yes, where the early morning is concerned, but when the Superior thinks there is weariness that demands more than seven hours' rest, he can give permission to retire earlier. 'But when they come in very late and are very tired?' In that case, there would be no harm in allowing longer rest in the morning, because necessity is its own rule. To think however, that illness will result from there being no intermission in observance is merely a fancy ; experience has proved the contrary. Since the rule was enforced, there has been no illness here or elsewhere that there was not before, and moreover we know, and the doctors repeat, that oversleep is bad both for the dull and the highly strung.

" Finally, if it be urged against me that there may be some reason which prevents somebody from going to rest at nine or ten o'clock, I answer that such reason must, if possible, be avoided. And if, there be impossibility, it will be so rare that the loss of an hour or two of sleep is insignificant compared with the harm done by one remaining in bed while the others are praying."

A number of his missioners were always at Saint Lazare, but a still greater number of them were away at branch-houses, which were now to be found all over France and even in several foreign countries. The task of controlling them was not easy, communications in those days being so difficult, and more particularly when the country was at war. The Superiors chosen for them also were in many cases quite young men, and although they might have been well trained by those responsible for their training at Saint Lazare, they were of necessity inexperienced in work which was often of considerable difficulty.

Vincent helped them as much as he was able, but they mostly stood in need of greater assistance than he could make available to them. " I acknowledge," he wrote once in their defence, " that the office of Superior in our houses is not always well filled ; but remember that in new-born communities this always happens. Grace follows nature in many things, and much that nature allowed to be rough and unpleasant at birth is perfected by time."

Here is sympathy for the lot of Superiors, but his reproof of them, when he deemed such necessary, was never withheld, and he could write thus to one who had flagrantly offended against the Rule. " I have been exceedingly astonished, and also distressed beyond power of expression, sir, by your conduct, and you must allow me to tell you that you have, ind   , done wrong."

Any rulings which he made as Father Superior he insisted should be followed without any questioning. " There is this difference between the opinion of an individual and that of the Superior General," he comments, " the first only sees and feels the things entrusted to him and is given grace only for that, while the goodness of God must give grace to the Superior General for the whole of the Company."

He kept always in closest touch with each member of the Congregation, and impressed upon the Superiors of the houses that those they ruled must be free to write to him direct at any time or under any circumstances. " In the name of God, do not check the most complete freedom in writing to the Superior General of any of those entrusted to you," he writes. "And do not imagine that anything is believed against a Superior without giving him a hearing, or that any action is ever taken on guess-work. I can assure you, sir, that I give no rebuke save on the testimony of the individual Superior himself."

Then turning to general reflections, which might be helpful to these often harassed men, he counsels : " Be on such simple, cordial terms with those under you that when you are all together, it would be impossible to say which is the Superior. Do not decide business of any importance without asking the advice of those you rule, and particularly that of your Assistant. For my own part, I always summon my colleagues when there is any difficulty to be decided, whether it be on spiritual or ecclesiastical matters, or on things temporal. Where these last are concerned, I take counsel with those who have them in charge. I take the advice of the lay brothers on the housekeeping because of their experience in it."

He was never tired of emphasising that the Superior should be " humble, gentle, kindly " towards those he ruled. " Though I do not mean that I always keep to this rule myself. When I break it, however, I know that I am failing." " How deep is human weakness! " he cries once. " Oh, what patience is needed to be a Superior! "

Branch-houses of the Congregation were to be found in such widely separated parts of France as Sedan, Tréguier in Brittany, Annecy near Geneva, Richelieu in Touraine,

Marseilles, the last being the most important of any of the French houses because of its position as a sea-port and the numbers of galley-slaves imprisoned there. A hospital for them had been opened in 1643 and members of the Congregation looked after it and were responsible also for the guidance of a large and growing seminary, besides much of the mission work of the district round their house. Then these labours were immensely increased when in 1649 there was an outbreak of plague so terrible that all who could escape the city did so. "The condition of the hulks reached at this time," we are told, "a point of horror from which the imagination recoils. There was no one to perform the most ordinary offices for the dying or the dead." Vincent's missioners, of whom there were only four, laboured tirelessly and one of their number died.

This foundation opened a door to yet another field of labour—one of even greater difficulty and which lay outside France itself. Across the Mediterranean and facing Marseilles lay the continent of Africa, whose various northern countries were known then as Barbary. These were held by the Turks, who infested the sea—as Vincent himself knew well—plundering the ships which passed through it. They killed any on board who put up a fight, and led the survivors to a slavery which was in many cases so terrible that "death was longed for and greeted with joy." A contemporary writes that some twenty thousand slaves were thus held, and conditions were worsened for them by the fact that their captors were continually urging them to forsake their faith for that of Mahomet. And many did so.

It can be imagined how deeply such a state of affairs would stir Vincent as he heard of them. Old memories of Tunis would be revived in him, and he accepted with delight a request, which came at last from Louis XIII at the close of the latter's reign, that he should send priests to Barbary for "the corporal and spiritual assistance of Christian captives." The King gave Vincent money for this end and the Duchesse d'Aiguillon, to whose generosity the opening of the house at Marseilles was largely due, asked to be allowed to share in the work. But it was one of extreme difficulty, the Turks being on the alert to prevent anything that would undermine their power. Vincent, however, was not easy to defeat, and he had presently arranged that each of the French consuls, attached to the various sea-ports along the North African coast, should have a priest of his Congregation for chaplain, and through these chaplains the slaves were reached. After a little time chapels were set up for their use, while the behaviour of the missioners during an outbreak of plague—similar to that of Marseilles—at one of the ports increased the power which the latter had already won.

" We have a great harvest in this country," wrote one of them to Vincent, " and it has grown even greater on account of the plague. For, apart from the Turks who were converted to our Faith, and whose conversion we kept secret, there are many others whose eyes were opened at the hour of death, and who have recognised and embraced the truths of our holy religion." He goes on then to describe one Frenchman, who having become a Moslem, died at length in penitence, " holding a crucifix to his breast. His wife, who also had denied the faith and who was once a professed nun, has likewise been absolved from her two-fold apostasy, having manifested all the necessary good dispositions."

Eight missioners were here, then no fewer than seven of them died of plague. Their house had been requisitioned at once as a hospital, the streets all round it being so filled with dead and dying, a contemporary tells us, that it was difficut to avoid treading on them. Six thousand of the inhabitants died each week, it was computed, during the period of the outbreak.

But such successes were balanced often by tragic failure, and Vincent's own wisdom in dealing with these foundations has been held in doubt. His eagerness at one time for the work of salvation to go forward prompted him to permit his priests to hold secular appointments—a move which was unpolitic and which brought disapproval from the Vatican.

North Africa was a far cry from Paris, but even further was Ireland, to which missioners set forth in 1645 at the request of the Sacred Congregation in Rome. Their task there was primarily to teach the correctness of the sacred ceremonies and rites to the clergy " who," the Prefect of Propaganda wrote, " are totally ignorant, owing to the long period of time in which the public exercise of the Catholic religion has been hindered by the heretics who are the masters of the country."

Eight or nine men were chosen, of whom five were Irish, and Vincent bade them a specially tender farewell, for their work, he knew, would be difficult and their journey fraught with danger. They started from Nantes and encountered, indeed, storms so fierce that they were nearly shipwrecked. But arrived in Ireland, they were warmly welcomed by the Archbishop of Cashel and the Bishop of Limerick in whose diocese they presently started to work. They preached, instructed, gave missions, then in 1648 all save four returned to France, those who returned being Frenchmen.

They had no settled house in Ireland, and as the work they had been sent to do was finished, they were anxious to be back in Paris. But the four Irishmen, who had accompanied them, were equally anxious to remain for a little while longer in Ireland, and this they were permitted to do. Their services were to prove valuable, for August of the following year brought Cromwell to Dublin, and thereafter savagery swept the land. He returned to England during the spring of the next year, but the country was not at rest, and June of 1651 saw the start of the siege of Limerick, in which one of those remaining missioners from Paris was tortured, then massacred " before his mother's eyes."

The country was considered thereafter to be subdued, but war and famine had made it derelict. Wolves prowled within a few miles of Dublin in their search for human flesh, there being no other flesh on which to feed. Practise of the Catholic faith was still forbidden, and priests could carry out their ministry only by disguising as laymen, and it was in disguise that two of the three last members of Vincent's Congregation slipped back to France. The fourth of the little band elected to stay behind, and he died in the country of his birth.

The work they did in Ireland won much appreciation. " I have often written to your Reverence of the labours of your missionaries in this kingdom," the Bishop of Limerick wrote to Vincent. " They are of such a nature that never within the memory of man, so we have heard it said, was there such good progress and advance made in the Catholic Faith, while

for myself, I confess, that I owe the salvation of my soul to
your children." It was suggested to Vincent that a history
of this Irish venture should be written, but he forbade it.
" It is enough," he said, " that God knows the good which
has been done. Our little Company should honour the hidden
life of Jesus Christ."

A similar mission was sent later to Scotland, where much
work was done amongst the natives of the Isles. Then in
1651 five missioners were despatched to Poland, whose Queen
was a Frenchwoman and a great friend of Mère Angélique
of Port Royal.

All these many projects demanded the services of a number
of men, and in some cases of a number of lives as well. But
the call which Vincent answered to start a foundation of his
Congregation in Madagascar made the most costly demands
of any. It was so costly in lives, indeed, and in suffering too
that one is tempted often to wonder—as many wondered at
the time—if Vincent were wise to continue with it.

The island, situated off the south-east coast of Africa, had
been annexed in the previous reign by Richelieu, who was
anxious to enlarge the colonial empire of his country. It was
quickly occupied by French settlers whose lives were anything
but edifying. The natives were idol-worshippers and quite
happy in such worship, so that when at length Vincent's
missioners reached their destination, no welcome was accorded
them. The climate was so bad that one after another
succumbed to it, while the distance from France was so great
and posts so fitful and long-delayed that on two occasions
death had carried off all the missioners, and the mission had
been left vacant for some years before Vincent had any
knowledge that all was not well with it. The sea claimed
the lives of several men.

" Somebody in the Company may remark," Vincent was
provoked to write one day, " that Madagascar should be
abandoned. Flesh and blood may say that no more men
should be sent there. Yet would it really be possible for us
to be so cowardly as to abandon this vineyard of the Lord
merely because four or five or six have died ? Would that
not be, indeed, a fine army, which because it had lost two or
three, or four thousand men abandoned the fight! Let us

say the same of the mission. Would it not be a fine Company, indeed, if because five or six have died, we were to abandon God's work ? "

And so, the disciples being worthy of their master, more and more volunteered for this most hazardous venture. And at Vincent's death, his successor in office continued it, knowing how near it had been to Vincent's heart. In 1674, however, the whole project had to be abandoned owing to the departure of the French colonists from the island. But it was resumed later when conditions became gradually so much better that Sisters of Charity were able to go out and share in the work.

Thus did Vincent rule his large and scattered Congregation with strength and gentleness, as well as with great serenity ; but above all, with a warmth and depth of love which was unfailing. Yet deep though his love for it was, he found the burden of its guiding so great that even so far back as 1642 he asked to be released from his post as Superior General. It was only at very real cost to himself that he consented at last to resume it, the whole Congregation having come to him in a body beseeching him to do so. He continued it then to the end of his life. Only death released him from it.

CHAPTER XIV

Life at Saint Lazare

SAINT LAZARE had become by this time one of the best-known houses in Paris. Every poor person in the city was familiar with it. Many members of the Court visited it, while it was used more and more by ecclesiastics. Bishops, who were visiting Paris, often craved its hospitality, while many strangers to the capital, or foreigners desiring instruction in the Faith asked to be received and were mostly admitted.

The vast edifice was ruled of course by Vincent, and no change in it was ever made without his knowledge. All the accounts passed through his hands, and they were of a most complicated order. Enormous sums of money were entrusted to him for distribution amongst the many charities he controlled. Money also had to be delegated to the various branch-houses of the Congregation, and always there was the care and upkeep of Saint Lazare itself. Several hundreds of people were catered for there each day. Numerous retreats were held beneath its roof, besides conferences and meetings, while the building being so old, was in constant need of repair. Complaints often occur in Vincent's letters of the amount of money which these repairs alone required.

The food provided for its many guests was always good and plentiful, this being a point to which Vincent gave some care. " I hear that your bread is not well baked," he wrote once to the Superior of a French house. " I beg you to have it made by a baker if you can find one, for it is most important to have good bread. Vary your food occasionally, so as to comfort poor human nature, which grows disgusted at always seeing the same things."

Saint Lazare was noted for the good manners of those who ruled it, and Vincent could note almost with complacency—"At Saint Lazare persons salute one another on meeting, and address each other hat in hand."

The large church attached to the building was open to the public and was famous for the beauty of its services and the perfection of its singing. Members of the Court often came to it, the Queen had been known to attend it, and it was used also by the inmates of Saint Lazare, though they had as well their own private chapel where Mass and Offices were said daily. The poor, whose demands were unending, were given every sort of assistance, even to gifts of shrouds in which to wrap their dead.

A small asylum for the insane had formed part of the old Saint Lazare, and Vincent continued the work which it had started. He found time to take a personal interest in the inmates, with whose affliction he always had particular sympathy. He accepted youthful delinquents too, who would be sent to him by their parents or on the order of a magistrate. " Our Lord chose to be surrounded by madmen and idiots, by the tempted and the possessed," he wrote. "And if He received them, shall we not receive them also ? "

Vincent's cell, where he spent so much of his life, differed little from any other in the building. It had neither mats, nor fireplace, nor curtains, we are told. Its furniture was a table, two chairs and a bed, the last consisting of " a rough straw mattress, a quilt, and bolster." Opening off the cell was a draughty little room dedicated to St. Joseph, where he received visitors.

His day began with three hours spent in the chapel, when he would say Mass, some of the Offices and give himself up to that mental prayer whose importance he was never tired of emphasising. " Mental prayer is *the* great book for a preacher," he would reiterate. Several hours of work, which as he grew older was chiefly writing, followed before he sat down at last to breakfast at ten o'clock. This he shared with the community and the subsequent hour of recreation he enjoyed, for he was a good conversationalist, besides being by nature very social. Vespers and compline were next recited, after which he was occupied with visitors and correspondence, until supper, which was at six o'clock. There were more visits then to the chapel, more work and correspondence before night-prayers and the reading of points for meditation for the morrow. At nine o'clock all in the house retired to rest, though the light in his cell often remained unextinguished until far into the night.

Retreats, he considered, to be the most important work of the house, and although he did not conduct them himself during his later years, he supervised them closely. Usually six ordination retreats were held yearly, the conductors of which would be exhorted by Vincent to aim primarily at simplicity—an exhortation which was needed in a day when preaching was very artificial and diffuse. Jokes and witticisms were much admired, together with long quotations from the classics, chosen to reveal the learning of the preacher. Vincent would countenance none of this. The priests chosen by him to preach must be clear and practical in their expositions, "lofty and noble thoughts" found no favour with him.

It was not only ordinands, however, who made retreats at Saint Lazare. As early as 1633 parish priests had arrived at the Collège des Bons Enfants asking for the benefit of the exercise. Later at Saint Lazare bishops came, soldiers, working-men, while numbers also arrived for private retreats. And all received the same careful welcome as that given to the ordinands. Each one who was a newcomer would be interviewed on his arrival by a missioner and conducted to his cell, where every effort was made to put him at his ease. "For he may be nervous as to what is going to happen to him when he finds himself alone in a room," Vincent notes. "One should try, if one can, to mingle modesty, gaiety and graciousness." And only the fewest and most simple questions might be asked. Payment was never exacted. Soon retreats were so much sought after that some seven or eight hundred of them were made each year.

The value of them had largely become known through those Tuesday Conferences, which Vincent had instituted so early in his career in Paris. Members of the Conferences now boasted priests who were amongst the best known in Paris, and Vincent, aware of the value of their work, made a point of attending their meetings whenever it was possible for him to do so. He was as accessible to them as he was to his missioners.

The spiritual direction of souls, however, was a task which, as years passed by, he hesitated to undertake. He simply had not time, and there were other priests now in Paris sufficiently trained to be quite capable of the work. But the direction which Francis de Sales had left him of the Visitation nuns remained his responsibility, though he had tried to relinquish it some years before.

One of the rules of his Congregation was that members of it should not devote themselves " to the service of nuns," since they were dedicated exclusively to work amongst the poor. And for this reason, if for no other, Vincent asked at last that his resignation as Superior of Sainte Chantal's daughters might be accepted. And it was, but at the end of eighteen months he was asked to reassume it and so much pressure was brought to bear on him that he consented. He carried the burden of it then until his death, but it remained a burden. " For me it is a cross and the heaviest cross I have to bear," he wrote. For the work did not grow less with passing years.

Four convents of the Order existed in Paris, and he must visit them each year, interviewing all the sisters and novices, then addressing the whole community with words which were often recalled throughout the ensuing months. Numerous chapter-meetings must be attended, much business transacted, which provided—together with the supervision and often the direction of individual nuns and novices—work which was exacting.

He was beloved by the nuns, for an unexpectedly deep understanding of their difficulties was his, and he could sympathise, as few other priests in Paris could, with the scruples, doubts, temptations which can bring so much anguish to the enclosed Religious. " In my opinion," he wrote, " there is nothing more important than to help such souls." He could be hard with them. " Nuns are dead to the world," he would say, " and should no longer recognise any earthly relation." A Visitation nun wrote once—" He had a marvellous skill in humbling haughty spirits, and did so as if he was just conversing at recreation. If Sisters had disobeyed in a serious matter, he reprimanded them in such a way that his admonition filled them with shame."

A deep devotion to Our Lady, which grew deeper as the years passed by, was always his, and was perhaps the reason partly for the reverence and respect he gave to women. To many women also he gave a close affection, which he was never afraid to show. Nor did he ever think to hide how much he could lean upon a number of them. At the close of a long letter to Sainte Chantal in which he had submitted to her the Rule of his Congregation for her opinion, he wrote—"You will have the charity, my dear Mother, out of love for Our Lord, to give us your opinion on it, if you please, and you may rest assured that I shall receive it as coming from God, out of whose love I ask this charity from you."

Her love for the Congregation was something which he greatly treasured, and he delighted to regard her as its mother. "How sovereignly you are our honoured and most loved Mother! You are so to such a degree that there is no word that can express it, only Our Lord Himself can make you feel it in your dear heart . . . most honoured Mother, more amiable and loved than I can express." And his affection for her she returned. "To whom can I reveal and make known my weaknesses if not to you, my one and only father," she wrote to him. "I trust that your goodness will not grow weary of them." Her soul, Vincent commented, was one of the holiest he had ever known.

Yet he gave an even deeper love to Louise de Marillac, who shared more widely and more profoundly all his interests. He and she were united in the closest and yet the holiest of bonds. So much of his work could not have been done without her help, as we have seen, while her debt to him was beyond reckoning. He had found her scrupulous, unhappy, a prey to morbidity and melancholy. Under his guidance she grew to be one of the great, even if still the least known, saints of history. He developed all her latent gifts, helping her to use them in ways which made her an instrument of inestimable value to the world.

Much of his correspondence with her remains, but we have few of his letters to Sainte Chantal. He was a prolific letter-writer, his letters being often very long and always diffuse in style. The thought of polishing anything he had written would never have occurred to him, for there was nothing of the artist in him. He seems to have been unaware of beauty or ugliness in his surroundings. Music alone of the arts stirred him, and that only in so far as it added to the decorum of religious services. His whole mind was bent, to the exclusion of all else, on God and the things of God. It is not surprising, therefore, to find religion almost always the sole topic of his letters. Simply, directly, with extraordinary lucidity he explains it, though wrapped round sometimes with so much repetition and occasional over-emphasis on the obvious that the reader can grow weary.

His correspondence was enormous and became more so when he was working for the Council of Conscience. All his activities in Paris—the foundlings, the Sisters of Charity, his work in hospitals and amongst galley-slaves, his organisation of retreats and the care of his Congregation—entailed innumerable letters. He wrote, we are told, during every moment he could snatch. He even wrote letters in the street and quite often in his jolting carriage. He wrote far into the night, his handwriting showing sometimes that he must have been fighting with sleep while his pen was in his hand. Then at last in 1645, when the Fronde was at its height, he was induced to employ a secretary, who presently employed in his turn an assistant.

The draughty little waiting-room which opened off his cell was seldom empty of people arrived to interview him, and those who came were of the most diverse. After 1650 many Irish priests were to be found amongst them, for following Cromwell's campaign, numbers of them fled their country to find shelter at Saint Lazare. They did not prove easy inmates there, however, for they were mostly so ignorant that work was difficult to find for them, while they objected to any sort of discipline or training. It was easier to ask for alms in the streets than to work, and the efforts made by Vincent and the Irish members of his Congregation to help them provoked only resentment and hostility. Of the numbers of Irish citizens who followed them to Paris, many of the men found they could get a living by joining the army, while for the women and children, a pitiful crowd " barefooted and covered with rags, who straggled through the streets looking for food and often contenting themselves with what the dogs had disdained to eat," Vincent invoked the aid of the ever-generous Ladies of Charity, who did not fail to give it.

The burdens laid upon him, as his life advanced, grew ever

greater, and each one, as it came to him, he shouldered quietly, deliberately, slowly. His slowness never changed. One eager request to him brought the reply—" I will think it over, but before doing so, I will examine the matter before God for a month, thereby to honour the silence which Our Lord so often observed when He was on earth." " Nature causes trees to take deep root in the earth before they bear fruit, and even then they do so very slowly," he would explain. " Our Lord acted in like manner in His mission upon earth, for He led a hidden life for a very long time before manifesting Himself and devoting Himself to the work of our redemption." " Divine things come into existence of themselves," was another axiom. " True wisdom consists in following Providence step by step."

The irritation which such seeming procrastination and delay could cause to others can be well imagined ; but Vincent never changed his methods, having proved their wisdom far too often. " I have never yet seen anything spoiled by my slowness," he once remarked, and on the rare occasions when he did take hurried action, such action failed, as we have seen, and he regretted it. " Leave all to God," still formed the keynote to his life. " Our Company began without any idea of ours," he liked to emphasise when referring to the Congregation, " and it has multiplied by God's guidance alone, without our having contributed anything but holy obedience. Let us go on acting in the same way. God will be best pleased with such abandonment and we shall be at peace. The spirit of the world is restless and eager to do all things, we will leave that spirit alone."

Yet if he demanded abandonment from those whom he ruled and directed, he demanded prudence also. A state of pure passivity he did not favour, but rather one of personal indifference, in which expectation must play a part, " the mind being ever on the alert to discover the indications of Providence, and the will prepared to carry them out." Thus might each soul become, indeed, a tool of God. " The affairs of God are accomplished little by little and almost imperceptibly. The spirit of God is neither violent nor hasty. God always gives a greater blessing to humble beginnings than to those which start with a chiming of bells."

The teaching which he had learned long years ago from de Bérulle—that of a personal identification in all things with the Son of God—he never forgot. He, who ruled so many things and people, was ruled himself exclusively by the Redeemer whom he loved. All the advice he gave, everything he did, every decision that he made was referred to Him alone. " You will honour the tranquillity of Our Lord's soul by a perfect acquiescence in the Divine will." " Ever hold in honour the passivity and the hidden state of the Son of God." " Why should you not weep? The Son of God, did He not weep for Lazarus? " " The gentleness of your disposition needs a tiny drop of vinegar. Borrow a little of it from Our Lord, who knew well how to find the bitter-sweet when it was needed."

Such was de Bérulle's exalted doctrine translated by Vincent into the language of every day, while side by side with it was his own shrewd, practical approach to every problem laid before him. " Before coming to a decision he sought for information and prudently weighed the reasons for and against," writes one of his sons of the present day. " If he was offered an establishment, he made enquiries to find out if the revenues were sufficient for the maintenance of the priests or sisters who were being sought for, and if disputes or law-suits might be involved." He would inquire further as to the nature of the work and if it was suitable to the capacities of those whom it was suggested should undertake it. " He would take counsel with God in prayer, and then with wise and prudent persons. If the work proposed to him seemed to have all the marks of one desired by God, then he accepted it."

Spirituality and intelligence thus went side by side to produce results which remain to the present day. And year after year he was unflagging in his work. Even by 1656, the year which saw the taking of life-vows by his Congregation, and when he himself was seventy-five, he showed no slackening. His body—of which he had always asked so much—might be wearing out, but his spirit was as eager and as active as it had ever been. Four more years of life remained to him. Death did not come to him until the autumn of 1660.

CHAPTER XV

The End

HE had always been strong in health, yet he had experienced frequent pain throughout his life. That old injury to his leg, which he had received from the Turkish pirates, had never cleared up, and the pain it caused increased as the years passed by. It was very severe at times.

He, who loved walking, had been obliged to give up the exercise not long before he went to Saint Lazare; he rode then on any missions which he took. Soon, however, even riding had to be relinquished, and by 1655 he was so crippled that he could go about only with the aid of a stick. Four years after he was unable to reach the chapel of the house. Then a moment came when his swollen, ulcerated legs refused to support him at all. He could not stand upright, so was debarred from saying Mass; he might only assist at it and receive Communion. His sufferings by then were often acute, more especially if he moved. " O Saviour! My dear Saviour! " he called out sometimes; but when inquiries were made of him, his reply was nearly always the same—" Our Lord suffered more than I do." Any remedies suggested to him he was ready to try, " purges, blood-lettings, sweatings." Delicacies sent to him by the Duchesse D'Aiguillon and others he would always accept, and he followed carefully any advice given to him by Louise de Marillac.

The spring of 1660 saw her death following an illness of many months. Her sufferings were greater than Vincent's own; an old injury to her left arm had brought on gangrene.

The Motherhouse of the Sisters of Charity was quite close

to Saint Lazare, as we have seen, and, as Louise's end approached, the thoughts of the old friends, so near and yet so widely separated, wandered constantly to one another. Vincent waited eagerly for reports of Louise. " She has fallen so ill," he wrote at the beginning of the year, " that we do not dare to hope for her recovery, and this greatly afflicts us."

Some months had passed since the two had met, when he wrote that, and a still longer time since Vincent had been able to give any of those conferences to the Sisters of Charity which it had been his joy to give. But he remained in close touch with the girls, and knew that as many of them as were able were flocking back from the country round to say goodbye to the mother whose death, it was evident, could not be far distant.

It was during the February of 1660 that she had become so gravely ill. She could not rise from her bed then, but lay all day in her little room. Then an operation produced a momentary rally and Vincent could write to one of the Sisters, who had not been able to get to Paris, that she was better. " It was necessary to make three large incisions in her left arm. She suffered a great deal, as you may imagine. The fever has now left her, but she is not as yet completely out of danger, because of her age and weakness. Everything is done to try and preserve her." Her fever and pain had returned, however, less than a week after that letter was written, and it was known then that the end was very near. She lingered, nevertheless for several days.

Many Ladies of Charity came to see her, while numbers of Sisters of Charity were continually beside her. " I cease not to ask God's blessing upon you all," she said to them, " and I pray that God may give you the grace of preserving you in your vocation in order to serve Him in the manner He asks of you. I beg of you to take the Blessed Virgin as your only Mother."

She had always hoped that Vincent would be with her at the moment of her death. This was now impossible, for although he could transact business, he could hardly move. Then at last she sent a message to him asking him if he would write to her. He could have done so quite well, yet he refused, and sent her instead only a few words by one of his priests.

" You are going the first," he said, " and if God pardons my
sins, I hope to rejoin you presently in heaven."

The words were not what she had hoped for, yet they
perhaps did not surprise her, for here was just the underlining
of a lesson which he had never tired of teaching her—and all
the other souls he guided—that she was to depend on God alone.
Only in Him lay peace and freedom. And hard though his
conduct may appear, it shows, nevertheless, how deep was his
regard for her. A weaker soul he would not have treated so ;
but his trust in her was so great that he confidently left her
to travel without his aid the last bit of her long journey.
And his trust was not misplaced. She received his message
with " extraordinary tranquillity." She died at last on Passion
Sunday, March 15, 1660.

The news of her death was brought at once to Vincent, who
said little as he received it. She had always been something
of an inspiration to him, and he seems to have had from the
first moment he learned of what had happened a definite sense
of her nearness to him. " I recommend her to your prayers,"
he wrote immediately to one of his missioners, " though
perhaps she has no need of them, as we all have reason to
hope that she is enjoying now the glory promised to those
who have served God and the poor in the manner she has
done."

An account of her death he sent at once to all the various
Sisters of Charity scattered over France, then during July he
waived aside the rule which forbade women to enter the
enclosure of Saint Lazare, and held one of those familiar
conferences for the Sisters in a large room not far distant
from his cell.

Many of the girls were crying, and he was not ashamed to
shed tears himself. Louise was the exclusive subject of the
conference, and as the Sisters spoke of her virtues, Vincent
listened, then added one which he had found of such inestimable value—her prudence. The word may have meant to
him something which we would now describe as judgment.
" Prudence, Sisters, prudence in all things. You will resolve
to practise this virtue earnestly all your lives, and ask our
good God for His assistance. And God will give it to you
if you ask Him for it for love of her, because although we

should not pray in public to the dead who are not canonised, we may pray to them in private. You may then ask prudence from God by her intercession." The Sisters met again in the same room on two subsequent occasions, and the Ladies of Charity met there also once to discuss and receive a final set of rules.

Vincent's missioners were now, as ever, often with him, while he remained in constant correspondence with those who were away. Then one day he came in contact with a member of his own family. A nephew of his arrived unexpectedly at Saint Lazare to see him.

For years he had been out of touch with all of his relations. His last reference to his mother is contained in a letter written fifty years before. That home, which he had visited last when he was still living with the de Gondis and which he had wept to leave, was never mentioned by him. He had reduced detachment to it to such a degree as is difficult to understand, for he was more than once reminded of it by others. One of his own priests, who had been holding a mission near it, spoke of its members to him once, describing their poverty with considerable compassion. "All they have to live on is the fruit of their labours," he said. To which Vincent replied—"And are they not very happy to be in such a state? Did not God say to man : ' Thou shalt earn thy bread in the sweat of thy brow?' " And to another who urged him to do something to help them, he was equally adamant in his refusal. " Do you think I do not love them? " he inquired. " I have all the affection for them that any man can have for his own. And I would hasten to assist them were I to follow the natural course of my feelings, but I am bound to think about the poor, who are most abandoned, and not about those who are bound to me by friendship and blood."

Here is the relentless logic which we have noticed before in Vincent, but there may have been something else as well—a little touch of pride in regard to these poor relations. He was always accusing himself of pride, which those who lived most closely to him never believed that he possessed. They saw him as the selfless mission priest, and one who was ready to accept with quiet dignity the insults which were often heaped upon him when he was at Court, and who was always so eager to take advice from all. Where was the pride of which he wrote and spoke so much?

He had revealed it years ago when as a brilliant youth at Dax he had been ashamed to acknowledge his relationship to his poorly dressed, peasant father. His peasant birth was something which he minded then acutely, and he minded it possibly always, his constant references to it being made in an effort to conquer something which he knew to be a weakness. And this knowledge it may be true to say—though all unconsciously—prompted his treatment of his relations, which treatment astonishes us today just as it astonished those who witnessed it.

He set his face always against giving his family any help, and would not even give one of them who wanted to be a priest any encouragement or even advice, which was actually all the latter wanted. Certainly shame as to his lowly origin was never wholly conquered, for at the end of his long life it swept over him with sudden force as a message was brought to him one day that his nephew—or more likely his great-nephew—was awaiting him downstairs. He was so surprised then that he was taken off his guard, and ordered at once the young man to be brought up to him by the back staircase. For would he not be poorly dressed and obviously a peasant? How could he appear to be anything else, seeing he had come straight from that distant Gascon farm?

Then in a moment he repented. The order was scarcely given before it was rescinded. What had he done? Succumbed to pride so elementary that he was ashamed to acknowledge his relationship to this poor man? His shame was so great that somehow he managed to totter from his room and down the stairs to receive his guest as though that guest was the greatest in the land. He embraced him, introduced him to all the members of the house whom he could find, telling them that this new arrival was the finest member of his family. He humbled himself, indeed, so continually before the youth that the latter was so much embarrassed that he left Saint Lazare as quickly as he could. And he left with a heavy heart and empty pockets. For he had come with the idea of extracting money from Vincent, and Vincent had refused to help him even with his fare back home. And

Vincent felt no sorrow for this conduct, which seems so regrettable to us, while he never ceased to repent his sudden little burst of pride, confessing it several times before his whole assembled congregation.

By the beginning of 1660 he was so crippled that it was suggested the room next to his own should be made into a chapel. He refused. Then, as the year wore on and his weakness grew, he gave his consent to the change, and heard Mass there for the first time on August 15.

The ulcerated condition of his legs was now spreading over his whole body, and great pain, besides extreme discomfort, were continually his ; but his mind was so lucid that he could still deal with his correspondence, grant interviews and advise about business. It was only when the full heat of summer came that his grip began to weaken. Long nights, in which continuous pain kept him wakeful, made him so that he dropped asleep quite often through the day. " I am suffering a little from my poor legs," he wrote on July 16. " They will not allow me to rest by night or walk by day, or even to stand upright. Apart from that, I am pretty well." But those who were closest to him knew that he was failing rapidly.

The pain was so great now when he lay down that he sat mostly in his chair. He was seventy-nine, and by the beginning of September it was realised that his end could not be distant. His cell, which used to be a centre of so much activity, had grown very quiet then. Its windows were often open, and one wonders as he sat with the sounds of Paris coming up to him if his mind ever travelled back—as the minds of old people so often do—to his youth and the years which had followed after—the farm where he had tended cows and sheep, then that tingling time at Dax and later at Toulouse, when he had absorbed knowledge and learned his own capacity for command and leadership.

His period of slavery in Africa was something of which he never spoke, but he could not have forgotten it, nor yet those early years of struggle in Paris which ended in the happiness of the little church at Clichy. To remain its curé always had been his dream, while long years with the de Gondis had been his lot instead, followed by the sudden freedom to Saint Lazare.

He had seen much history from behind its walls and had played a certain small part in it himself. There was his watch by the bedside of the dying Louis XIII, the affection for him of the Queen, his contact with the Court and with the two Cardinals who ruled it each in turn. Mazarin still dominated the Court and had arranged a short while previously a marriage for the young king—now a handsome youth of twenty—with the Spanish Infanta. Paris has been *en gala* during the spring to celebrate it. The Cardinal himself, however, was now facing the same death which was nearing Vincent. It would come to him the following year. The two had been brought so closely together by those terrible years of war. Now war had retreated from the capital and peace was reigning—a peace which would not last for long.

Peace had played little part in the pattern of Vincent's life. Warfare had made the principal background of it. Yet he himself had always known great peace, and peace was folding him closely now as he waited for the end. His periods of wakefulness became less frequent as September advanced. He just drowsed through the days. " Brother sleep has come," he whispered once, " and is waiting for his sister death." The sister was approaching fast.

The day before he died was a Sunday and he was taken then to Mass in the room beside his cell, and there he received " for the last time the Bread of life that fortifies and sustains." He fell asleep the moment he returned to his cell and slept quietly through most of the following day and night, rousing himself only to receive Extreme Unction and to give a blessing to the Congregation, the work of Saint Lazare, the Ladies of Charity, the Sisters of Charity, the foundlings and all his friends.

The weather must have turned cold before the evening, for we read of a fire having been lighted in his cell and seated over it he died at last just before five o'clock on the following morning, September 27, 1660. There was no struggle. He just slipped peacefully away with an expression of such " beauty and majesty " on his face as astonished all who saw it.

He was buried the next day in the church of Saint Lazare, which was far too small to hold the crowds which flocked to it to pay their reverence to him.

His beatification followed sixty-nine years after, though many had begun to ask his prayers already. The story of his rich, unfailing love was not likely to be forgotten, and still today his memory remains—fadeless and undimned—even though nearly three hundred years have passed since that September morning when his tired body found its rest.